20th Century Defences in The East Midlands

Derbyshire, Leicestershire, Lincolnshire, Northamptonshire, Nottinghamshire and Rutland

Mike Osborne

CONCRETE PUBLICATIONS

Published by Concrete Publications

45 Church Street
Market Deeping
Lincolnshire
PE6 8AN

British Library Cataloguing in Publication Data:
A catalogue record is available from the British Library.

ISBN 0 95403781 2

Printed by
Biddles Ltd
Guildford and Kings Lynn

Dr Mike Osborne has lived and worked in the east Midlands for nearly 30 years. Having taken early retirement, he spends his time researching military structures, and has published several works on English Civil Fortifications and 20th Century defences. He is currently working on a book on 20th Century military remains across the whole of Britain, and is in the process of carrying out a fieldwork survey of Drill Halls and TA Centres. He is a longtime member of the Fortress Study Group, and the Airfield Research Group. He was a volunteer Area Coordinator for the Defence of Britain Project from its start in 1995, covering ten eastern counties from Lincolnshire to Oxfordshire.

Front cover illustration: A F C Construction or Oakington pillbox at Grafton Underwood, Northamptonshire.

CONTENTS

ACKNOWLEDGMENTS

Thanks are due to the following, in no particular order: David and Margaret Sibley, tireless and generous fieldworkers; Adrian Armishaw has kindly contributed material, as ever, including the piece on Sywell, and read through the manuscript for me; the daughter of the late Henry Meir for getting his work to the DoB Project archive. Harry Thorpe and family of Pingley PoW Camp. Jeff Dorman, for permission to use his drawings of Haile Sand Fort. Nick Catford's work on underground structures generally, and his report on Watnall in particular, must be mentioned here. Norman Nichol's listing of WWI PoW camps is indispensable. Graham Cadman, Archaeological Conservation Officer for Northamptonshire has, as ever, been generous and helpful in sharing information and ideas; Derby Local Studies Library, Leicestershire Record Office, and Nottinghamshire Archives, for unearthing Defence Plans. Terri Sansom for setting up the text, and supervising the production process; John Downey of Market Deeping for consistently processing my photographs; my wife, Pam, who has spent large chunks of the last 35 years, trekking round derelict fields searching for lumps of old concrete, and seeking out, and finding, obscure documents in archive offices and libraries.

ABBREVIATIONS USED IN THE TEXT

AA Anti-aircraft
AAOR Anti-aircraft Operations Room
AM Air Ministry
AML Air Ministry Laboratory, as in synthetic bombing teacher
ARP Air-raid Precautions
AT Anti-tank
BHQ Battle Headquarters, airfield defence
BL breech-loading [gun]
BOP Battery Observation Post
BSA Birmingham Small Arms
CASL Coast Artillery Searchlight
CH Chain Home
CHEL Chain Home Extra-Low
CHL Chain Home Low- all Radars
DEL Defence Electric Light
DEMS Defensively Equipped Merchant Ships
DL Defended Locality
FAD Forward Ammunition Depot
FDL Forward Defence Line [Summer 1940]
FIDO Fog Investigation Dispersal Operation
FWD3 [War Office] Fortifications & Works Department 3
GCHQ Government Communications Headquarters
GCI Ground Control Interception
GHQ General Headquarters [Line, 1940]
GDA Gun-defended Area
GPO General Post Office
GS General Service [hangar]
H/LAA Heavy/Light anti-aircraft
IRBM Intermediate Range Ballistic Missile
LMS London Midland Scottish & LNER London North-Eastern Railway, both [pre- Nationalisation] railway companies
MAFF Ministry of Agriculture, Food & Fisheries
MAP Ministry of Aircraft Production
MOWP Ministry of War Production
MT Motor Transport
MU Maintenance Unit [RAF]
NFE night-flying equipment
NFF National [Shell] Filling Factory

OP Observation Post
O[C]TU Officer [Cadet] Training Unit [Army]
OTU Operational Training Unit [RAF]
PAD Permanent Ammunition Depot
PoW Prisoner-of-War
QF quick-firing
QRA Quick Reaction Alert
RA Royal Artillery
RAF Royal Air Force
RAOC Royal Army Ordnance Corps
RASC Royal Army Service Corps
RDF Radio Direction-Finding
RE Royal Engineers
REME Royal Electrical & Mechanical Engineers
RNAS Royal Naval Air Service [later Fleet Air Arm]
ROC Royal Observer Corps
RML Rifled muzzle-loader [gun]
ROF Royal Ordnance Factory
RSG Regional seat of government
RSJ rolled steel joist
SAM surface to air missile
SL searchlight
SMLE Short Magazine Lee-Enfield
S-RC sub-Regional Control
TA Territorial Army
TAC Territorial Army Centre
UKWMO United Kingdom Warning & Monitoring Organisation
USAAF United States Army Air Force
USAF United States Air Force
VCR Visual Control Room
VHF very high-frequency
W/T wireless/telegraphy

INTRODUCTION

Only in the last few years, has any real interest in the military structures of the 20th Century, been shown by other than specialist enthusiasts, belonging to such organisations as the Fortress Study Group [FSG] and its off-shoots, and the Airfield Research Group [ARG]. In 1995, following a pilot study in Holderness by the FSG, the Defence of Britain Project [DoB] was set up to identify and record 20th Century military structures across Britain. This involved most of the major heritage organisations, and large numbers of volunteers, who submitted records to a central database, now on the Internet.

Many known sites were located within a wider context, and Colin Dobinson's documentary research informed new fieldwork. A clearer picture began to emerge of defence works embracing the Victorian age of gunpowder, through two World Wars, the Cold War, to the era of Star Wars. One unfortunate fact to be highlighted by the fieldwork, was the rapidity with which these sites are disappearing. After the 1918 Armistice, defence works were destroyed, for there would never again be any future need for such things. In 1945, most local authorities had clearance programmes to remove obstructions and perceived eyesores. The general post-war reconstruction, and the ephemeral nature of many of the structures themselves, accounted for clearance, replacement and natural decay. The turn of the century has seen this process hastened by a combination of circumstances. The end of the Cold War and successive Governments' wish to reduce defence-spending, has coincided with a desire, motivated by concerns for the environment, to meet the increased need for new housing, by building on brown-field sites. The end result is the accelerated destruction of many military sites - airfields, defence works, camps etc. Fortunately many, but by no means all, of these structures have been recorded. Some, moreover, have been given a degree of statutory protection. Sadly, it is possible to gauge this accelerated destruction with some specific examples. Since this present writer's book on Lincolnshire was published in 1997, the blockhouse at Sibsey, the defended WIT station at Manby, the World War I gun-towers at Killingholme, the Watch Office at Fulbeck, the triple coupled GS hangars at Bracebridge Heath, the home-guard store at **Dodwsby**, and all but the original CH structures at Stenigot, have been demolished. This book, one of a series, originating from the early days of the Defence of Britain Project, attempts to sample the **rant** of structures which existed, and to Point to surviving examples in the six counties of the east Midlands. There will undoubtedly be undiscovered structures from this period out there. The author would be delighted to be informed of new finds, as would the appropriate County Sites and Monuments officers.

Please note that many of the sites recorded here, are on private land, and the appropriate permissions must be obtained prior to a visit. Even then, care must be taken on, what are often, dangerous sites. The other titles in this Series are, KENT by David Burridge and LINCOLNSHIRE by Mike Osborne both published by Brasseys in 1997, and CAMBRIDGESHIRE by Mike Osborne published by Concrete Publications in 2001.

errata p. ix
line 5 “Dowsby”
line 8 “range” not “rant”
line 9 “point”

1 AIRFIELDS IN THE EAST MIDLANDS

The Army Manoeuvres of Autumn, 1913, were held in the south Midlands, with the defending force, the White Army, based in Northamptonshire at Daventry. For the very first time, the aerial dimension was involved, and a mixture of 20 aircraft, based on Lilbourne, operated in a reconnaissance role, for the White Army which was staging a strategic withdrawal, using forward landing grounds at Towcester and Badby, until over-run by the advancing Brown Army. Lessons, soon to be put into practice for real, were learned, and military aviation was about to take its place on the real battlefield. In both World Wars, the East Midlands accommodated a wide variety of military airfields. These included landing grounds for fighters, airship and seaplane bases in World War 1, and the whole range of operational, training and support bases in the World War II.

AIRFIELDS IN WORLD WAR I

In 1916, bombing raids by Zeppelins, prompted the setting-up of Home Defence Squadrons. This was to supplement the Royal Naval Air Service [RNAS] squadron based at Killingholme [Lincs.] One, No.33 Squadron, was based at Scampton, Kirton-in-Lindsey, and Eisham [Lincs.], and No.38 Squadron, at Melton Mowbray and Buckminster [Leics.] and at Leadenham [Lincs.]. Lilbourne and Easton-on-the- Hill [Northants.] operated as training stations. Also in 1916, Cranwell [Lincs.] was established as an, aircraft, airship and balloon training centre by the RNAS, and it soon proved necessary to expand into Digby and Freiston [Lincs.]. The Admiralty fuel depot at Killingholme, was defended by a RNAS balloon centre at Immingham [Lincs.]. Hucknall [Notts.], Harlaxton, South Carlton, Spitalgate, Waddington, and Hemswell [Lincs.], all opened as training airfields at

HUCKNALL [Notts.]. Coupled General Service Sheds, 1917. Two pairs survive in commercial use; two further pairs, used by Rolls Royce, have gone.

this time. The home defence fighters found difficulty in staying up long enough to intercept the Zeppelins, so a network of emergency landing-grounds was established to provide a safety-net. These included Greenland Top, Swinstead, Willoughby Hills, Tydd St Mary, and Market Deeping (Lincs.]. Aircraft Acceptance Parks were built at West Common, Handley-Page Field, and Bracebridge Heath, all in Lincoln, to receive the output of the City's aircraft factories. The officers' mess of the West Common site was in the Grandstand of the Racecourse. At Loughborough [Leics.] the Brush Aircraft factory had its own airfield for flying off newly-built aircraft. From 1918, US flyers were based at Killingholme, and many received training at Waddington. Lilbourne [Northants.] finished the War as a school for flying instructors.

Many of these airfields had quite significant structures, most of which have long disappeared. Aircraft, at this time, were very vulnerable to bad weather, so tended to be kept under cover. Canvas Bessoneau hangars were widely used, but, as the War progressed, many airfields, and even the acceptance parks, received brick-built GS hangars, often referred

HEMSWELL [Lincs.]. Hipped C Hangar, one of four built in 1936. The top- of-the-range hangar found on many Expansion Period airfields.

to as Belfast Truss hangars, because of their roof construction. Two triples of this type have recently been demolished at Bracebridge Heath, leaving only the single aircraft repair shed standing. Two double GS sheds still stand at Hucknall [Notts.l. The side-opening F Shed, an Admiralty design, for housing seaplanes on RNAS bases, was, after the end of the War, used at some armament training stations. Two examples can be seen at Sywell [Northants], used in World War II for aircraft assembly. At Scampton, Digby and Waddington, the GS sheds were replaced by new hangars in the 1930s. At Scampton, the massive airship shed, 700' [215 m] by 150'[46 m] by 100'[31 m], two smaller sheds, and the wind screens, 700'[215 m] by 70' [21 m], each end of the big shed, have all gone. At Tydd St Mary [Lincs.], the small, brick flight hut, the predecessor of the control tower, still remains. One semi-ruined building stands at Leadenham, but, otherwise, virtually everything from this period has gone.

RE-ARMAMENT THE EXPANSION PERIOD AIRFIELDS OF THE 1930s.

By the eariy-1930s, it had become apparent that, despite the war to end wars, European conflict was again a strong possibility. Re-armament is visible in our region in two respects. Firstly, the growth of civilian flying, which increased the pool of trained pilots, and, secondly, the construction of the infrastructure; airfields and depots which would allow a modernised RAF to operate. Also significant was the general expansion in civil aviation which encouraged the growth of municipal airports out of civic pride.

NEWTON [Notts.]. Austerity or Protected C Hangar, 1938, one of five. A similar group may be seen at Binbrook [Lincs.]

In 1927, Northamptonshire Aero Club opened at Sywell. Tollerton [Notts.] opened in 1929, and Nottingham Flying Club moved in two years later. Waltham [Grimsby] opened in 1933 as the home of Lincolnshire Aero Club, it ultimately became a bomber base. Braunstone [Leics.] opened as the proposed Leicester Airport in 1935, but was leased to Leicestershire Aero Club. In 1938, a RAF training school opened on what was briefly, Derby's city airport at Burnaston. By

POLEBROOK [Northants.]. Type J Hangar, 1939. These were cheaper and quicker to build than the C Types hitherto used on permanent airfields.

this time, Sywell, under civilian management, and Tollerton were already training RAF aircrew, whilst Braunstone was to become a satellite of the RAF flying training school at Desford [Leics.]. At Sywell, the club-house, hangars etc. remain from this time. Waltham is still an airfield. Braunstone has been sucked into Leicester's suburbs, Tollerton is Nottingham's airport, and Burnaston has disappeared under Toyota's works.

Dwarfing these civilian developments, was the RAF Expansion Programme. A large number of new, or improved, airfields were built to house the strategic bomber force, which was the mainstay of defence policy. Once more, the RAF's planners saw the Lincoln Cliff as the best jumping-off point for bombers raiding across the North Sea. Existing bases such as Waddington, Scampton, Kirton-in-Lindsey, Spitalgate, Hemswell, Cranwell and Digby [Lincs.], were up-dated with new buildings. New airfields were built at Manby and Binbrook [Lincs.], Cottesmore [Leics.], and Newton [Notts.]. These airfields were very much products of peace-time. Their buildings were designed to plans approved by the Royal Fine Arts Commission, and the Council for the Preservation of Rural England. Predictably their style is an elegant neo-Georgian, with the odd touch of moderne. Cranwell's neo-Baroque of a few years earlier, is even grander. The most obvious buildings are the Type C hangars and associated aircraft repair sheds, still to be seen at all these stations. Spacious officers' and sergeants' messes, Institutes for the men, H-shaped barrack-blocks, armoury, HQ, sick-bay, MT-sheds, guard-room, workshops and stores, can all still be recognised, as they were universal on these stations. Watch-offices were often the 'fort' type [1959/34] as at Cottesmore, Hemswell, Digby, Scampton and Kirton-in-Lindsey. Waddington received its'villa'type [5845/39] a little later, replacing its earlier 'fort'. One concession to the possibility of hostile action on some stations, was the building of the hangars in an arc, in order to avoid destruction by a single stick of bombs. This can be seen at Manby, Newton and Scampton, for instance.

Opening by the end of 1940, another group of new airfields share most of the expansion period building designs, but differ in two respects. Here, the hangars are less substantial - the curved J Type [5836/39] rather than the C Type., and the watch office is often the 518/40, in temporary brick. Airfields in this category include Syerston [Notts.]; Chelveston, Chipping Warden and Polebrook [Northants.]. North Luffenham [Rutland]. Elsham Wolds, Coningsby, Swinderby and Goxhill [Lincs.]. The 518/40 continued to be built for some time, and later examples can be seen at Bottesford and Wymeswold [Leics.].

Other airfields opened during this run-up to War, but do not conform to either pattern just described. As armament practice camps, North Coates was given a double F Shed, and Sutton Bridge, the more usual ex-RNAS single F Shed. Burnaston [Derbys.], built pre-War as a civil airport had a Bellman hangar, supplemented under RAF management, with dispersed Blister hangars, and Waltham [Grimsby], another private airfield, had a non-standard hangar. From now on, things were to be different.

AIRFIELDS IN WORLD WAR II

Two criteria dictated the plan and appearance of airfields for the duration of the War – security and economy. The aesthetic went out of the [neo-Georgian] window. Neat, gridiron layouts of elegant buildings, instantly recognised from the air, did nothing to protect men or machines. Labour and resources were scarce, so utility buildings were needed, on dispersed sites. A new control tower, the 343/43 was designed to meet the needs of most types of airfield, and new hangars appeared - the T2, transportable, and erected on a steel frame, and the B1, developed by the Ministry of Aircraft Production, and used on operational airfields for the on-site repair of damaged aircraft. Most bomber stations, built after 1940, had 2 T2s and a B1. Some of the US 8th Army Air Force transport stations had more: 4 T2s at Barkston Heath [Lincs.], for instance. Blister hangars also made their appearance at this time and an example stands at Caistor [Lincs.]. There were also other control towers for specialist functions. Coleby Grange [Lincs.] has a 12096/41 for night- fighter stations, with additions; Kingscliffe [North-

LANGAR [Notts.]. T2 Hangar, 1942, designed to be transportable.

CHURCH BROUGHTON [Derbys.]. B1 Hangar, 1941, designed as an aircraft repair shed by the Ministry of Aircraft Production. Most bomber fields had a B1 and two T2s. This hangar is visible from the A50 road. A T2 stands nearby.

CAISTOR [Lincs.]. Over Blister Hangar, 1941, for storage of fighter planes.

CONINGSBY [Lincs.]. Gaydon Hangar, 1953, to accommodate V-bombers.

BINBROOK [Lincs.]. Quick Reaction Alert Hangar, 1972, for Lightnings.

NEWTON [Notts.]. 'Villa' type Control Tower, 1938, frequently found on Expansion Period airfields.

BOTTESFORD [Leics.]. Control Tower, a well-restored example of the Type 518140 tower found on airfields built around the start of World War II.

LANGAR [Notts.]. One of the last surviving examples in Britain of this bomber satellite Type A Control Tower. Waltham [Lincs.] retains its Type B tower.

LEICESTER EAST [Leics.]. A good example, in use since 1943, of the most common of the World War II utility Control Towers, the Type 343143.

WIGSLEY [Notts.]. The unique 3-storey Control Tower of 1942; there are three-deckers elsewhere but no other to this unknown design.

ants.] and Hibaldstow [Lincs.] have FCW4514 towers for night-fighters, and Woolfox Lodge [Rutland] has a Type 453213/43, also for night-fighters. Waltham and Ingham have Type 7345/41 for bomber satellite stations, as had Blyton [Lincs.]. Gamston [Notts.] and Bardney [Lincs.] have Type 13726/41 Grafton Underwood [Northants.] and Saltby [Leics.] both had Type 13079/41 towers as has Langar [Notts] still. The all-purpose Type 343/43 towers still stand at Husbands Bosworth, Bruntingthorpe and Leicester East [Leics.], Silverstone [Northants.], and East Kirkby, Sandtoft and Strubby [Lincs.]. The example at Ashbourne [Derbys.] converted into offices, was not visible on a recent visit, and may have been demolished. The three-storey tower at Wigsley [Notts.] is unique.

Apart from hangars and control towers, virtually all other buildings on war-time airfields were either temporary brick, or hutting, usually Nissen or Romney. Given the intended short life of these buildings, it is amazing how resilient many are, and how much survives. The control towers at

NEWTON [Notts.]. Parachute Store, 1938, a similar one is at Hemswell.

HUSBANDS BOSWORTH [Leics.]. Parachute Store, c1942, a typical example of this utility building found on most World War II airfields.

SILVERSTONE [Northants.] A double version of the AML [Air Ministry Laboratory] Bombing Teacher.

Gamston, Hibaldstow and Sandtoft have been converted to houses; Wickenby and Sturgate [Lincs.] still function as control towers – many hangars and huts are used for industrial, agricultural, or commercial purposes; and not a few continue in their original functions. A number of even these utility designs have their separate identifies. The gymnasium, with or without chapel extension [16428/40] can still be seen at Desborough [Northants.), East Kirkby, Metheringham and Goxhill [Lincs.], and Bottesford [Leics.], Ashbourne [Derbys.], and at Kingscliffe [Northants.]. Another distinctive building is the parachute store. Examples of Type 11137/41 survive at Husbands Bosworth, Bottesford and Wymeswold [Leics.]; this appears to be a refined version of Type 17865/39; and those of Type 10825/42 at Gamston [Notts.], Waltham, Sandtoft and Ingham [Lincs.] and Deenethorpe [Northants.], perhaps represent the final version. Operations blocks [4891/42] survive at North Witham, Spilsby and Metheringham [Lincs.] and Melton Mowbray [Leics.]. The Ops block at Harrington [Northants.] is now the Carpetbaggers Museum. Even the ubiquitous hutting

WYMESWOLD [Leics.]. Instructional building [No.41] of 1942, most probably for gunnery training.

SYERSTON [Notts]. Typical Expansion Period officers' mess.

NEWTON [Notts.]. Station HQ with attached Operations Block. Typical of many Expansion Period airfields, this set-up can be seen at Hemswell [Lincs.]

can sometimes be identified by its particular conformation. Hence Romney huts at Deenethorpe, Desborough and Spanhoe [Northants], can be seen as Main Stores and Main Workshops. Perhaps the striking contrast between the expansion period architecture, and the war-time building, is best exemplified by water-towers. The stylish, brick-clad towers of Manby or Hemswell seem of a different era compared to the starkness of the steel Braithwaite tanks, on their latticed, metal frameworks, at Metheringham or Wymeswold. However, these buildings did the jobs for which they were designed. During 1942, a new airfield, many of them in the East Midlands, opened every three days. As the Lancasters came on stream concrete runways were essential. During the War, the equivalent of 5000 miles (8000 km) of three-lane motorway was constructed. Airfield construction took up a third of all available labour. Each bomber base was a small town of 2000 people requiring services from, and frequently swamping, local communities. By 1945 our region

BINBROOK [Lincs.]. The elegant brick-clad Water-tower of 1940. Probably one of the last to be built to the standard set by the Royal Fine Art Commission.

WYMESWOLD [Leics.]. The in-your-face utilitarian Water-tower of 1942.

SYERSTON [Notts.]. The squash court behind the officers' mess.

ASHBOURNE [Derbys.]. Gymnasium/Chapel on the Communal Site now a caravan park; the officers' mess and squash court stand alongside.

had almost 50 operational bomber bases, some of them belonging to the US 8th Army Air Force. Additionally there were fighter bases, British and American, and the transport bases of the US 9th AAF, which would carry the paratroops to Normandy, Arnhem and the Rhine. Then, there were training bases, some of them very specialist like Burnaston for the Glider Pilot Regiment, and the hush-hush stations like Harrington dropping secret agents into France, and keeping them, and the Resistance, supplied. The FIDO system of fog dispersal was installed on four of Lincolnshire's airfields, at Fiskerton, Ludford Magna, Metheringham and Sturgate. A few of these dozens of airfields continued their work after the end of the War, but many reverted to agriculture, or disappeared under urban sprawl, and, on some sites, next to nothing remains to tell us what was once there.

RANGES AND OTHER ANCILLARY INSTALLATIONS

To keep the whole, vast operation at peak performance demanded co-ordination, training and practice. RAF bomber HQ in our region was at St Vincents, Grantham, [No.5 Group] from 1937, until its move to Morton Hall, near Swinderby, in 1943.

The HQ of fighter units was at Blankney Hall, near Digby, [No. 12 Group]. The HQ of 67th Fighter Wing, US 8th AAF, including Kingsciiffe and Goxhill, was at Walcot Hall, just outside Stamford. The Northamptonshire bomber bases of the US 8th AAF, lst Bombardment Division - Chelveston, Deenethorpe, Grafton Underwood and Polebrook, were all administered from outside the region. The HQ of Troop Carrier Command, US 9th AAF, was at Grantham Lodge, presumably St Vincents, when vacated by Bomber Command. The US troop carrier stations were Bottesford and Saltby [Leics.] Balderton and Langar [Notts.]; Spanhoe [Northants.]; Cottesmore and North Luffenham [Rutland]. Barkston Heath, Folkingham, Fulbeck, and North Witham [Lincs]. As well as the RAF Maintenance Units, detailed in Chapter 8, there were RAF Repair depots at Barnwell [Northants.], and Honington [Lincs.]. The RAF had hospitals at Nocton Hall and Rauceby

GRIMSTHORPE PARK [Lincs.] Bombing range quadrant tower.

[Lincs.], the former subsequently becoming a full general hospital until its closure in 1983, and the latter reverting to a mental hospital after the War. Nocton Hall is now a care home.

In World War I, bombing and firing ranges were close to airfields. During the inter-war years it was felt to be necessary to set up dedicated ranges which were distant and isolated. Lincolnshire's Armament Practice Camps at Sutton Bridge and North Coates utilised specialist ranges at Holbeach and Donna Nook, and later at Wainfleet and Theddlethorpe as well. The use of these ranges along the coast, continued throughout World War II, and, in some cases, up to the present. There were also bombing ranges inland. Bearshanks Wood, Shutianger and Preston Capes [Northants.], Ragdale [Leics], Mowsley [Rutiand]; and Bassingham Fen, Lea Marsh, Fenton, Grimsthorpe Castle, and Manton Common [Lincs.] all had ranges used by Operational Training Units [OTUS] of Bomber Command. There were inland gunnery ranges at Hamilton Hill and Roman, Hole [Lincs.]. Holmpton [Lincs.] was used for air-to-air firing by US fighter trainers, as was Kinder Scout [Derbys.] by air-gunners of 42 OTU based at Ashbourne and Darley Moor [Derbys.]. The US 8th AAF practised their high-level bombing at Breast Sands on the Wash. In the park at Grimsthorpe, and on a hillside at Preston Capes, are quadrant towers, used for giving instant feed-back to bomb-aimers.

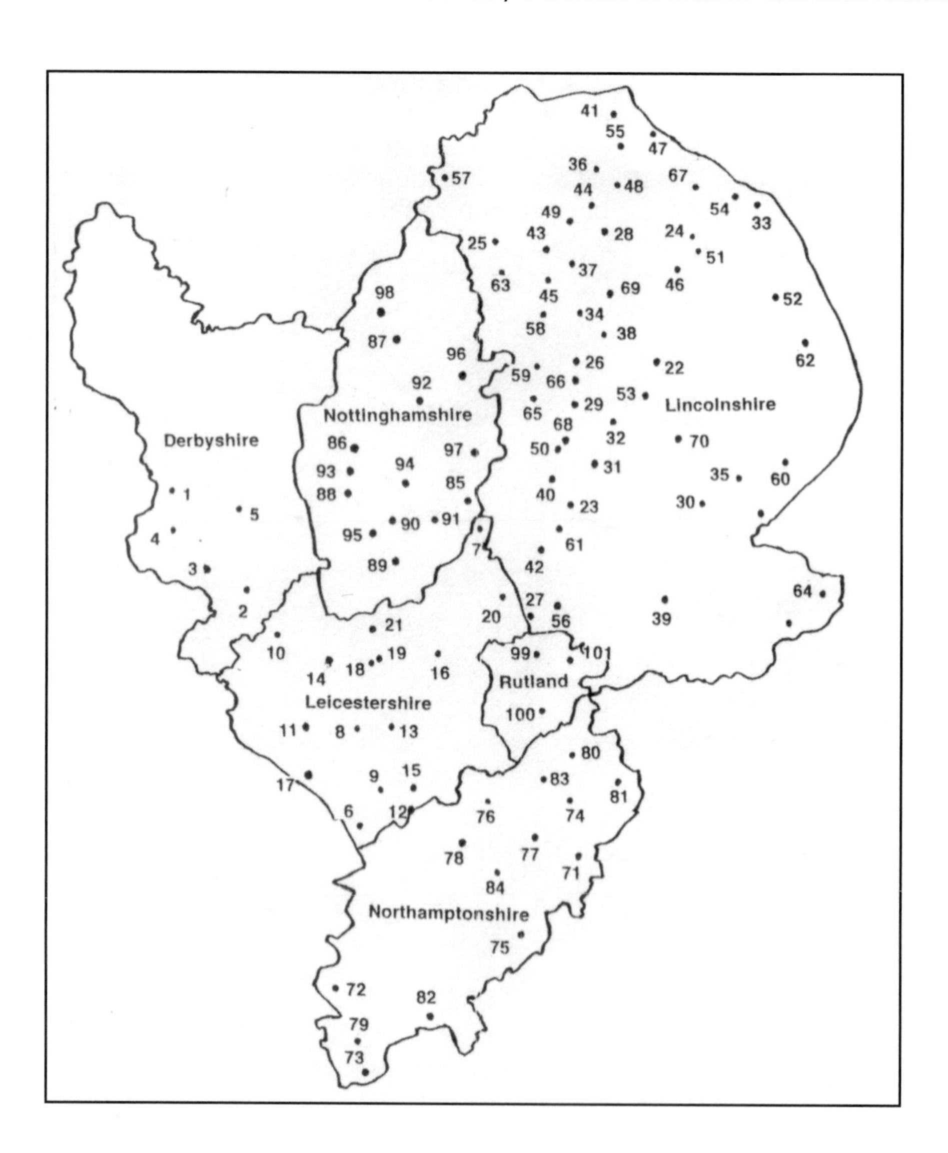

Airfields in the East Midlands.

AIRFIELDS IN THE EAST MIDLANDS

DERBYSHIRE

1 Ashbourne: WWII bombers; now Ind/Com;T2s+huts, gym, mess etc remain.

2 Burnaston: civil pre-War; WWII training; now site of Toyota works; no remains.

3 Church Broughton: WWII bomber OTU, & Rolls-Royce testing, now Ag; Bl +huts.

4 Darley Moor: WWII bomber OTU; now motor-cycle track; slight remains.

5 Hardwick Park: WWII SLG - restored to parkland; no trace remains.

LEICESTERSHIRE

6 Bitteswell: WWII bomber OTU; aircraft assembly; now Magna Park Distribution Centre.

7 Bottesford: WWII bombers, now Ind/Com. restored WO+T2s, many huts remain.

8 Braunstone: civil pre-War; WWII training; now Ind/Com-, few remains.

9 Bruntingthorpe: WWII bomber OTU; OW USAF; now vehicle testing; museum.

10 Castle Donington: WWII bomber OTU; now East Midlands Airport; few remains.

11 Desford: civil pre-War; WWII training, now Ind/Com., CRO hangar+clubhouse etc.

12 Husbands Bosworth: WWII bomber OTU; now Ag.+ Police Helipad; WO+Huts;

13 Leicester East: WWII glider-tugs; now Aero Club; WO+T2+huts remain.

14 Loughborough: separate WWI & WWII testing grounds; now Ind/Com.

15 Market Harborough: WWII bomber OTU; now Ag. & prison; BHQ+huts.

16 Melton Mowbray: WWII ferry units; THOR; now Ag/Ind/Com; THOR pads+huts.

17 Nuneaton: WWII bomber OTU; now vehicle testing; WO+T2+huts remain.

18 Ratcliffe-on-Wreake: WWII ferry units; now Ag; no traces.

19 Rearsby: 1938 through WWII aircraft factory; now Ag/Ind/Com; factory buildings.

20 Saltby: WWII 9USAAF transport; now private flying; huts remain.

21 Wymeswold: WWII bomber OTU; now Ind/Com; racing; almost complete layout.

LINCOLNSHIRE

22 Bardney: WWII bomber satellite; THOR; now Ag; WO + T2s.

23 Barkston Heath: WWII 9USAAF transport; now RAF; WO + T2s.

24 Binbrook: EP, WWII bombers, CW fighters; now housing; much remains.,

25 Blyton: WWII bombers; now Ag.

26 Bracebridge Heath: WWI & WWII; now Ind/Com; B1+ WWI Aircraft Repair Shed.

27 Buckminster: WWI landing ground; now Ag.

28 Caistor: WWII RLG; THOR; now AG; THOR pads remain.

29 Coleby Grange: WWII night-fighters, THOR; now Ag; WO+T2+THOR pads.

30 Coningsby: WWII bombers; CW fighters etc; now RAF; much remains.

31 Cranwell: WWI RNAS airships; RAF College, 1920 to present; complete.

32 Digby: WWI to present in RAF service; much remains.

33 Donna Nook: WWII ELG; now Range & Ag; slight remains of huts.

34 Dunholme Lodge: WWII bombers; CW Bloodhound SAMS; now Ag; remains.

35 East Kirkby: WWII bombers; now Air Museum., extensive remains, WO + T2 tec.

36 Elsham Wolds: WWI & WWII bombers; now Ind/Com; J Hangar remains.

37 Faldingworth: WWII bombers; CW PAD/ROF., now Com/Ag; B1+ PAD etc remain.

38 Fiskerton: WWII bombers; CW ROC HQ; now Ind/Com/Ag; huts+ ROC remain.

39 Folkingham: WWII 9USAAF transport; THOR; now Ag; THOR pads+ huts remain;

40 Fulbeck: WWII 9USAAF transport; now Ag; slight remains.

41 Goxhill. WWII RAF & 8USAAF fighters; now Ag- WO+J & T2, BHQ etc. remain.

42 Harlaxton: WWI & WWII training; now Ag & Ed; remains of huts.

43 Hemswell: WWI, EP, WWII bombers; THOR; now Ind/Com; extensive remains.

44 Hibaldstow: WWII fighters; now Ag+ gliding; WO is house, BHQ+ remains.
45 Ingham: WWII bombers; now Ag; WO+ huts etc remain.
46 Kelstern: WWI ELG; WWII bombers; now Ag; stand-by set house+ huts remain.
47 Killingholme: WWI RNAS & US flying-boats; no remains.
48 Kirmington: WWII bombers; now Humberside Airport; buildings modernised.
49 Kirton-in-Lindsey: WWI LG; EP & WWII fighters; now Barracks; much remains.
50 Leadenham: WWI LG.1 now Ag; fragmentary remains.
51 Ludford Magna: WWII bombers; THOR; now Ag, slight remains.
52 Manby: EP bomber station; WWII training., now Ind/Com/Admin; most remains.
53 Metheringham: WWII bombers; now Air Museum; many buildings remain.
54 North Coates: WWI & WWII coastal+training; CW SAMS; extensive remains.
55 North Killingholme: WWII bombers; now Ind/Com; T2s etc remain.
56 North Witham: WWII 9USAAF transport; now forest & Ind/Com. WO+T2.
57 Sandtoft: WWII bombers; now housing & Ag. WO + synthetic trainers remain.
58 Scampton: WWI to present in RAF use; complete EP airfield.
59 Skellingthorpe: WWII bombers; now housing; no remains.
60 Spilsby: WWII bombers; now Ag; B1+ops block etc remain.
61 Spitalgate [Grantham]: WWI & WWII training; now TA base; EP lay-out remains.
62 Strubby: WWII Coastal Command; now Ag; WO+BL +huts etc remain.
63 Sturgate: WWII bombers; now private flying, WO+huts etc remain.
64 Sutton Bridge: WWII gunnery training; now Com; hangars, butts etc remain.
65 Swinderby: WWII bombers; CW recruit training; now part housing; WOs+Js+EP.

66 Waddington: WWI training; 1926-present RAF; complete EP lay-out remains.
67 Waltham [Grimsby]: civil pre-WWII; then bombers; now Ind/Com; WO+B1+T2s.
68 Wellingore: WWII fighters, now Ag; defended dispersals+BHQ+pillboxes remain.
69 Wickenby: WWII bombers; now private flying; WO+hangars+huts+BHQ remain.
70 Woodhall Spa: WWII bombers; CW SAMS; few remains; Thorpe Camp museum.

NORTHAMPTONSHIRE

71 Chelveston: WWII 9USAAF transport & glider trials; now Ag. few remains.
72 Chipping Warden: WWII bomber OTU; now Ind/Com; J hangars, huts etc remain.
73 Croughton: WWII OTU & glider training" now US communications base;
74 Deenethorpe, WWII bombers; now Ag; parachute store; huts etc remain.
75 Denton: WWII RLG; now Ag; no remains.
76 Desborough: WWII bomber OTU, now Com; T2s+gym/chapel+huts etc.
77 Grafton Underwood: WWII 8USAAF bombers; now Ag, ops block, BHQ, huts etc.
78 Harrington: WWII bomber OTU & Carpetbaggers; THOR; now Ag; air museum.
79 Hinton-in-the-Hedges: WWII bomber OTU & airborne radio trials; private flying.
80 Kingscliffe: WWII RAF & 8USAAF fighters; now Ag; WO+PBX+sheiters+huts etc.
81 Polebrook: WWII 8USAAF bombers; THOR; now Ind/Com. J hangar,THOR pads.
82 Silverstone: WWII bomber OTU; now motor-racing; WO+trainers+huts etc.
83 Spanhoe: WWII 9USAAF transport; now Ind/Ag; many huts remain.
84 Sywell: civil pre-War; WWII training & aircraft production.
85 Balderton: WWII 9USAAF transport; now Ag; no traces remain.
86 Blidworth: WWII LG; now Ag; guardroom converted to bungalow.
87 Gamston: WWII bomber OTU; now Ind/Com/Ag; private flying; much remains.

88 Hucknall: WWI training; WWII fighters+Rolis Royce; now Aero Club+Rolls Royce.
89 Langar: WWII bombers & 9USAAF transport; now private flying; some remains.
90 Newton: WWII training; now Ind/Com; complete EP layout.
91 Orston: WWII training satellite; now Ag; no trace remains.
92 Ossington: WWII bomber OTU; now Ag; BHQ+huts remain.
93 Papplewick Moor: WWI RLG; WWII training RLG; no remains.
94 Syerston: WWII bombers, now RAF Gliding School; WO+J hangars+EP layout.
95 Tollerton: civil pre-War; WWII training; now Nottingham Airport; much remains.
96 Wigsley: WWII bombers & OTU, now Ag; unique 3-storey WO remains.
97 Winthorpe: WWII bombers; now Showground & air museum; some remains.
98 Worksop: WWII bomber OTU; now Ag+vehicle testing,, no remains.

RUTLAND

99 Cottesmore: WWII bombers & OTU; 9USAAF transport; CW V-bombers; RAF.
100 North Luffenham: WWII bombers & OTU & glider training, THOR; now Barracks.
101 Woolfox Lodge: WWII bombers & 9USAAF transport; CW SAMs; now Ag.

NOTES AND ABBREVIATIONS

Ag: agricultural use
Com: commercial use
Ed: educational use
Ind: industrial use
CW: Cold War
OTU; operational training unit
WO: Watch Office
ELG/LG/RLG emergency/relief landing ground
EP: Expansion Period
CRO: Civilian Repair Organisation
US[A]AF: United States [Army] Air Force

NB. buildings are sometimes moved around: one of the T2s at Desborough came from porington, and another from South Wales, possibly St Athan; one of them occupies the site of Desborough's B1. The pre-War hangars from Desford ended up at Tollerton.

2 COAST DEFENCES

The coast between the Humber Estuary and the Wash has always been seen as vulnerable to invasion across the North Sea. Whilst much of the responsibility for countering this threat has traditionally rested on the Royal Navy, land defences have also had a part to play. At the turn of the nineteenth-century, the port of Hull, and the Estuary of the Humber were defended by Victorian coast-batteries, some of them superimposed on even earlier fortifications. As coast artillery improved both in terms of range and power, then it became possible to have fewer guns, further away from the targets they were protecting. Thus the nineteen 64 pounder Rifled Muzzle Loaders [RML], emplaced by 1880, in Fort Paull opposite Stailingborough, with a maximum range of less than two miles, would soon be replaced by a smaller

FREISTON SHORE Coast Battery: engine-room, magazine and gunhouse.

FREISTON SHORE Coast Battery: Right-hand Gunhouse; the loops for musketry defence in the rear wall are visible.

number of 6" breech loaders [BL] nearer the mouth of the Estuary, covering arcs with a radius of up to 7 miles. By 1900, larger guns on the coast itself, could hit attacking ships up to twelve miles out to sea, so long as they could see them.

COAST DEFENCES IN WORLD WAR I

The port facilities of Hull were seen as the most likely target for enemy action. The heavier coast guns were therefore clustered around the mouth of the Estuary to prevent incursions by large warships, whilst batteries of quick firing [QF] guns were sited along the river to counter raids by torpedo-boats and fast motor-boats. Most of the batteries were on the north bank of the Humber and on Spurn Head, but there were guns on the Lincolnshire side. The battery at Killingholme had two 12 pdr. QF guns, each mounted on a 20' high, octagonal concrete tower, in order to clear the flood-bank behind which they were built in 1915. These were demolished, for no good reason, in 2001. A battery of two 6"

BL guns was built at Stallingborough, opposite two more, on towers, at Sunk Island. Their interlocking arcs of fire sealed off the river above Grimsby. The very mouth of the Humber was further closed to hostile traffic by two sea-forts, four storeys high, sitting on piles driven into the sandy sea-bed. Haile Sand Fort, located on the Lincolnshire shore, just off Cleethorpes, was started in May 1915, and, after two years work, was equipped with two 4" guns and their associated searchlights and range-finders. Whilst the threat of actual invasion had receded, small, localised raids or bombardment by enemy heavy cruisers, such as had happened further up the Yorkshire coast in late 1914, were still seen as real threats. Haile Sand Fort cost £0.5m, but came too late to be of more than psychological use. As well as the fixed defences, a 9.2" railway gun ran on track between Grimsby and Cleethorpes. The Royal Navy had a flotilla of destroyers as well as auxiliary craft, based in the estuary, some in the new port of Immingham, which had opened in 1912. One of the biggest threats came from enemy mines, and the majority of the Grimsby trawler fleet was occupied in minesweeping duties, or other tasks like servicing the Boom across the river-mouth.

Along the remainder of the Lincolnshire coast, pillboxes were built to defend the beaches. These were concrete blockhouses, with loopholes for rifles or machine- guns. The prototype pillbox was cylindrical, about 10' in diameter, and about 8' high. It often had a slightly over-hanging roof, making it look like the box you got your pills from at the pharmacy. According to contemporary photographs, and later maps of beach defences, those built on the Lincolnshire coast were generally hexagonal, similar to some built in France, behind the trenches. Liberal use was made of barbed wire, and, at night the coastal roads were closed by wire-barriers. Sentries kept a permanent watch, using public telephones for their reporting to HQ, two-hourly, through the night. Village postmistresses must have longed for an uninterrupted night's sleep. Units assigned to coast defence duties were constantly having to provide replacements for casualties on the Western Front. Many positions fortified in World War I would be re-fortified in the next war. Conse-

FREISTON SHORE Coast Battery: the Coast Defence Searchlight emplacement at the extreme right-hand edge of the site.

quently, since so many have been damaged, it is difficult to differentiate between the concrete emplacements of the two periods. There may be unrecognised pillboxes from World War I still in existence. However, cosmetic improvements to the coastline between the wars, coastal defence works, and erosion, have all taken their toll. Zion Hill at Theddlethorpe is known to have had a machine-gun post on its summit, but erosion has radically altered its profile in the intervening years.

COAST DEFENCES IN WORLD WAR II

Following the debacle of Dunkirk in May 1940, the country was, once again, facing the strong probability of imminent invasion. The strategy adopted by General Ironside, C-in-C Home Forces, was more-or-less forced on him. Despite a current gospel of mobility, deeply embedded in military planners since the horrors of static trench warfare, circumstances made this impossible to achieve. With few tanks, anti-tank guns, or trucks, Ironside had little alternative but to adopt a defence based on fixed fortifications. Having witnessed the Blitzkrieg in France, he at least attempted a defence in depth. The first of these layers was to be, what he called the "Coastal Crust". His intention was to delay invading forces on the beaches, in order to make time for mobile reserves to be brought up to counter attack. Such reserves, equipped with the only tanks and modern artillery in the country, were held at rail-heads, ready to be deployed as, when, and where necessary. As the factories produced more tanks, trucks and guns, then the strength, mobility and numbers, of these forces could be increased.

The Coastal Crust consisted of a number of elements. Established coast defence batteries were supplemented by emergency batteries, and beach defence guns; in this way, the entire invasion coast was covered by artillery. The beaches were mined, and had anti-landing obstacles - continuous barriers of tubular scaffolding, and lines of anti-tank blocks, all, just above the normal high-water mark. All the way along the crests of the dunes and other dominant features were concrete machine-gun emplacements, sited to provide inter-locking fields of fire over the beaches. Beach exits were blocked with anti-tank obstacles, and a further line of pillboxes ran parallel to, and up to half-a-mile inland from the coast. Observation posts were set up to overlook the beaches, and networks of trenches, weapons-pits, barbed-wire entanglements, and more mines, completed the defences. This can be clearly seen in maps of the Anderby area, drawn up c1946 to help plan demolitions.

ARTILLERY IN THE COASTAL CRUST

All the above elements were present on the Lincolnshire coast in 1940. The south bank of the Humber already had two established batteries from World War I, at Stallingborough, which exchanged its two old 6" guns for a pair of slightly newer naval 4.7" guns in covered gun-houses, and an unchanged Killingholme. Haile Sand Fort received two Twin 6 pounder guns. These were designed to counter fast motor gunboats and could reach a rate of fire of 40 rounds-per-minute from each barrel. Teamed with two further pairs

FREISTON SHORE. Coast Battery, unusual close-defence pillbox with open light-anti-aircraft position on top; TF397425.

on Bull Sand Fort, this presented a formidable obstacle to the E-boats preying on coastal shipping. Some indication of the effectiveness of these weapons is given by a night action in Malta, in 1941, when five Italian torpedo-boats were sunk inside two minutes. According to the official record, emergency batteries were built at Grimsby Docks, Mablethorpe, Gibraltar Point, and Boston. These each consisted of a pair of ex-Naval 6" BL Mark VII guns, from store, having been salvaged from scrapped World War I cruisers. They were mounted in concrete emplacements, with the whole gun on its pedestal, and with its shield, fastened onto its holdfast with 20 bolts. Behind each gun-house was a two-part magazine for cartridges and projectiles. Flanking the position were two Coast Artillery Searchlights [CASL] in open-fronted, shuttered emplacements. A battery observation post [BOP], office, generator building, and battery-charging hut, all defended by pillboxes, completed the front line on the Seabank. Behind, were all the huts for administration, accommodation, workshops, stores etc. necessary to service the needs of a 200-strong gunner unit. Although almost all the ancillary buildings have gone, the business end of

SKEGNESS, observation post overlooking the beach; TF570642.

Freiston Shore battery- the Examination Battery for the port of Boston, still remains well-nigh complete. Before the War, horse-races were run on the sands here, and a pair of hotels had been built for race-goers. It is possible that the top floor of Plummers Hotel provided a platform for the battery's Barr & Stroud range-finding equipment. Boston was an Examination Battery, so the Navy would escort suspect merchantmen to anchor under the guns, until cleared to proceed. It was therefore manned by regular troops well into the War. Many coast batteries were manned by the Home Guard, after the threat of invasion had become less acute. Of the other emergency batteries, little remains. At Gibraltar Point, the remaining CASL emplacement has been turned into a bird-hide. At Jackson's Corner, to the north of Skegness, the gun platforms and engine-room of a battery stand in the Yacht Club compound. This location does not appear in the record until late in 1941. At Mablethorpe, the battery has disappeared without trace, but its location is well-remembered locally. Of Crook Bank, not a fully-fledged emergency battery, but, nevertheless, a pair of emplaced heavy weapons ex-Naval 4" guns, only the close-defence pillbox, and concrete platforms survive. A similar site for a single 4" gun stood at Horseshoe Point until the 1980s. Here, a small [B]OP still stands, along with a loop-holed infantry block-house. Similar [B]OPs, originally accessed through tunnels in the dunes, standing at Tetney and on Skegness seafront, may have doubled as mine-watching posts. Last of the fixed artillery defences were the beach defence guns. These comprised a number of positions such as Pyes Hall, Red Farm, Seaview Farm, Howden's Pullover, and Fishtoft, armed with ex-Naval 6 pounder Hotchkiss QF guns, first used as saluting or anti-boarding guns on Edwardian Dreadnoughts, and then brought out of store to be fitted into male World War 1 tanks, built, incidentally, in Lincoln. Some of these beach defence positions can still be seen. At Fishtoft, near the Port of Boston beacon, behind what was once The Jolly Sailor PH, is a gazebo, built around a 6 pounder gun-house. Another, more easily recognised, stands at Pyes Hall. Sadly, there has been much indiscriminate demolition, first in the 1950s to restore a holiday coast, and, more recently, in the name of health and safety. Fortunately, Freiston Shore remains, and now that the reclaimed land in front of it is being returned to nature, the sea may once again lap below the gun-houses.

MOBILE ARTILLERY

Mobile guns were more numerous than the fixed. There were the heavier 4" and 12 pounder guns mounted on lorries, and dozens of old US 75mm guns mounted on wheeled carriages, to be towed behind cars and vans. For a while, a battery of four new 25 pounders was emplaced inland from Mablethorpe, but they were obviously considered to be under-utilised there and were soon moved on, to a more threatened area. Mobility was also achieved, as in World War I, by using railways. At Whitton Ness, Stailingborough and Grimsby, 12" rail-mounted howitzers, probably some of the batch reconditioned at the Derby locomotive works, were stationed as extra cover for the vital Naval fuel installations on the south bank of the Humber. The Guards Brigade defending this sector in May 1940, put together an armoured train, with steel-plate-reinforced sides and roof, and firing loops, further strengthened with concrete, for the protection of Grimsby. Later in the year, railway designers, including Sir Nigel Gresley of the LNER, met at Kings Cross Station, to plan a fleet of purpose-built armoured trains for the defence of the East Coast. Each consisted of a locomotive in the middle, a drop-side wagon fore and aft, and an open, fighting truck at each end. Armament was two 6 pounder Hotchkiss guns, Lewis guns, Bren-guns and Boys 0.55" AT rifles. Train 'M' patrolled Lincolnshire's coastal lines, spending time based at Louth, Boston and Spalding.

Throughout the War, as priorities, tactics, and available resources changed, guns were redeployed between locations. By mid-1941, the War had spread world-wide, and the Navy desperately needed guns to arm vulnerable merchantmen, so many guns, borrowed in 1940, were returned.

PILLBOXES AS BEACH DEFENCES

Every half-mile, or so, along the Lincolnshire coast stands a pillbox. At many points they are much closer together than this. Where there are beach-exits, they are combined with

THEDDLETHORPE-ST-HELEN. Local adaptation of Type 23 pillbox with two covered chambers and open platform for LAA gun; TF475891.

BOSTON DOCKS. Type 23 pillbox overlooking the river; TF327433.

AT blocks. There appear to be about three basic blockhouse types. The most common throughout the region as well as along the coast is the simple hexagonal Type 22 pillbox. This was a design originated by the War Office's Fortifications & Works Department 3 [FWD3]. It is a regular hexagon in shape, with walls 15" [37cm] thick. In each of five faces is a rifle-loop, splayed to the outside. The sixth face contains a doorway, with, generally, one pistol-loop, to one side. In the middle of the pillbox, is a Y-shaped, anti-ricochet wall. These Type 22 pillboxes are particularly prevalent along the Seabank south of Freiston Shore, astride the coast road at Wrangle, and around Hogsthorpe. Much of the immediate inland line is made up of these. A particularly tastefully landscaped example can be seen outside a factory at South Ferriby.

In the centre of Boston are three standard FW3 Type 23 pillboxes. These have a square, covered chamber with three loopholes, and an open, rear pit with a post mounting for a LAA machine-gun. Much more common, however, is a local variation, [FWD3/23 Lincs.] found only in Lincolnshire, which adds a second, covered chamber, the other side of the open LAA position. Roughly forty examples of this type survive, on the coast alone. One near Theddlethorpe is camouflaged as a pig-sty, another in Mablethorpe formerly had a false roof and painted windows, as a chalet, and a third, at Sutterton, in the graveyard, had headstones painted on it. There are a number of examples where the pit has been roofed over to form a two-chambered rectangular blockhouse. One example at Warren House, has a large, beach-flanking, heavy machine-gun embrasure in one end.

Another structure, almost unique to Lincolnshire [there is one example in Tees-side], is a rectangular blockhouse with a door at each end, flanked by a loop, and three loops in each long side. By each door is an open pit, some of which are for mortars, and others for LAA machine-gun mountings. About a dozen of these survive around the Wash.

Apart from these most frequently-seen types, there are FWD3/26 square pillboxes, and variations; a Type 22 with an open upper floor with LAA mounting, Type 22s at Gibraltar Point and near Sutton Bridge, with integral porches, and a split-level blockhouse near Boston. Strangest, are the half-dozen pillboxes near Saltfleet which are designed to look like rocky outcrops. One has masked loops which enfilade the beach. Others now have holdfasts on their roofs. Could they be recycled World War I structures? One, at least, at Warren House, built in rusticated cottage style, has another pillbox [Type FWD3/23 Lincs.] built right in front of it.

THE ROYAL NAVY IN LINCOLNSHIRE

Clearly, coast defence was only one minor element of the Navy's brief, but in the dark days of autumn 1940, it was a case of all hands to the pumps. Immingham and Grimsby were both important naval bases. At Immingham, HMS Beaver II, was established in 1939 for rescue tugs, and HMS Beaver III, in 1942 as a coastal forces base. In Grimsby, the Pekin Dock building housed the naval offices, Heneage Road, naval sick-quarters, and the docks held dozens of minesweeping trawlers and auxiliary patrol boats. Sutcliffe

HAILE SAND FORT. North-east [top] & south-west [bottom] elevations of the fort, as completed at the very end of World War I. [Jeff Dorman]

Buildings held the HQ of the DEMS - the armed merchant ships organisation. Butlins, Skegness was requisitioned as HMS Royal Arthur in September 1939, and served out the War as an initial training centre. The Navy completed the building of the Gaiety Theatre, now, in imminent danger of demolition, and maintained the famous chalets, one of which is still preserved, for the duration. They housed over 250,000 'hostilities only' ratings during the War. Billy Butlin was compensated for his loss of earnings on the basis of his 1939 season. At Boston, HMS Arbella, named for a daughter of the Earl of Lincoln who sailed with the Pilgrim Fathers, was naval HQ for the anti-submarine defences of the Wash. It was located in the Workhouse, part of which survives near the docks. The Sheaf Iron Works in Lincoln became a Royal Naval Armaments Depot, and there was a RN Medical Depot at Huthwaite, near Mansfield [Notts.].

The improvised coast defences were not tested, and after Hitler's invasion of Russia in 1941, it became less and less likely that they ever would be, although the German forces earmarked, were not re-assigned until February 1942. Neither did the British Chiefs of Staff committee, charged with second-guessing the Sealion planners, cease meeting until well into 1942.

FREISTON SHORE, BOSTON, LINCOLNSHIRE EMERGENCY COAST DEFENCE & EXAMINATION BATTERY

The battery consisted of two ex-Naval 6" BL guns mounted in brick and concrete casemates. The guns, from scrapped WWI cruisers, were mounted, with their shields, on hold-fasts, with 20 bolts, set into the concrete apron. The gun had an arc of fire of nearly 180 degrees, with elevation from −10 degrees to +16 degrees. The gun fired a 100lb [44.4kg] shell to a maximum range of 14000 yds. [12925 m]. Each gunhouse was linked, by a ramp, to its magazine, behind a wall, loopholed for rifles. Here, the magazines are above ground, but below the sea-bank on which the battery is built. Each magazine has three separate compartments for shells, cartridges and fuses. Steel shelves held the shells, but the inflammable cartridges were stacked on wooden ones. The battery consists of two CASL emplacements, close-defence pillboxes, an engine-room, office/crew-room, and battery-charging room. The BOP may have been on the top floor of the adjacent hotel. All of the numerous huts have gone, but a wartime, brick building, possibly a garage, stands by the road-side.

Boston Examination Bty. The Right-hand Gunhouse for Mk. VII 6"BL Gun

An examination battery was one where the Navy could escort suspect merchant ships to anchor within range of the guns until cleared to enter port. The two guns, here, nos. 1190 & 1245, were installed and ready for action by June 1940, manned by 320 Bty. 545 Coast Defence Regt. RA., and, in 1943 until late 1944, by 437 Bty. Boston Examination Bty.

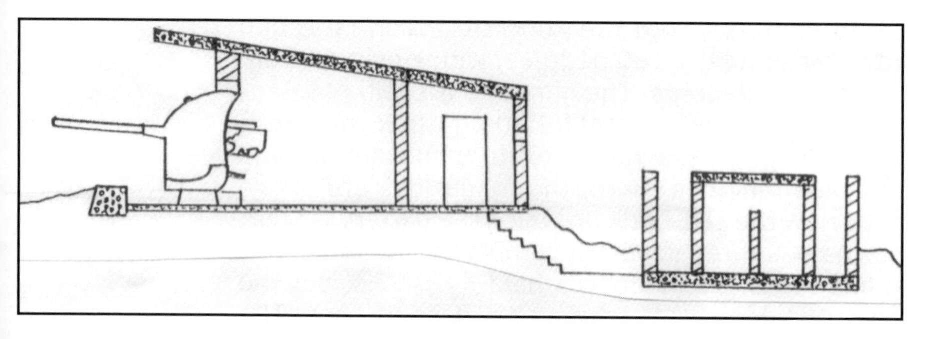

Cross-section of a 6" gunhouse and magazine

3 DEFENCE LINES IN THE EAST MIDLANDS

As we have seen, the Coastal Crust was only the first of the linear positions taken up by the defending forces in Autumn 1940. The key defensive line was always envisaged as the General Headquarters [GHQ] Line, or, as it was originally named, the Forward Defence Line [FDL]. Between this Line and the coast, local defence lines were designated- but not necessarily developed. Behind the GHQ Line, the mobile reserves were concentrated for any necessary counter-attack. A further line of defences, runs along the western borders of our region from Tamworth to Burton along the rivers Tame and Trent, then along the Dove to Uttoxeter and Ashbourne.

THE GHQ LINE IN THE EAST MIDLANDS

The GHQ Line was planned as a continuous anti-tank obstacle, utilising natural features in the landscape, strengthened by concrete blockhouses, wire, mines and fire-trenches, as a barrier against invasion forces. The Line in Southern Command has all these characteristics, but, at the point on the River Welland, near Crowland [Lincs.] where it crosses into Northern Command, this all changes. The route as far as Bourne [Lincs.] is straightforward, and follows existing drainage channels, but from there, the FDL Reconnaissance Report of June 1940, is in two minds. Overall, a route to the east of the A15 road - past Morton, Rippingale, Folkingham and Heydour, then swinging off west to Barkston on the River Witham, was preferred to a more westerly route which would have followed streams to Ropsley, and then joined the Witham a little earlier. Although there might have been less digging to be done, too much of the proposed Line would have been dominated by higher ground. Thus, the higher, easterly route was adopted. From the Witham to the

STICKFORD [Lincs.]. Type 28a emplacement for 6 pdr. Hotchkiss QF gun sited to fire across the fen towards the Hobhole Drain; TF351582.

Trent at Winthorpe, the river, itself, would provide sufficient obstacle once it had been deepened, and the bank scarped. Alternatively, the railway could be followed, but, here, a new, parallel ditch was recommended by the engineers. From Newark, north to the Humber, the Trent was more than adequate as an anti-tank barrier. it is impossible to tell how much, of this, if anything was built. There is certainly very little on the ground. On 30 June, the order had been given in 44th Infantry Division Operational Instruction No.3, to construct a full defensive scheme between Gainsborough and Selby. A week later, an order was issued to cease work on pillboxes, unless they were almost complete. It would appear that priorities were elsewhere when labour and materials were scarce. If an invasion was on the way, it was less likely to be at the end of one of the longer, and more dangerous sea crossings. Although designed only to be manned in the event of an invasion actually taking place, the GHQ Line, in the southern half of the country, at least, was very much a significant fortified barrier to an enemy's progress. In Lincolnshire and Nottinghamshire, it was little more than a line on a map. Where the integral waterways constituted an actual barrier, then demolitions were set up on the bridges crossing them. Some to be detonated as soon as the emergency was confirmed; others to be held for troop movement, only to be blown at the last possible moment. In August 1940, 209 and 213 Field Coys. RE, were ready to blow the bridges over the Trent at South Muskham, Fledborough, Dunham, Torksey, Gainsborough [2] and Althorpe [2]. Later, in mid-1941, the plans changed, and certain bridges were to be retained and defended. Possibly the sockets for AT rails, still visible on Torksey railway bridge, date from this time. Both main bridges at Gainsborough were defended by AT obstacles, by 1941, as part of an all-round defence of the town. Whilst the strategy might have been sound, the reality of the situation was dire. The GHQ Line was weak in Northern Command, and the reserve striking force available for a counter-invasion thrust was tiny. With its HQ at Guilsborough House [Northants.] 2nd Armoured Division with around 180 light tanks, armed only with machine-guns, and the motorised 43rd Infantry Division, with minimal artillery support, was, until the end of 1940, all that stood between the forward troops near the coast, those holding the Line, and the wide-open Midlands.

DEFENCE LINES IN LINCOLNSHIRE

In order to slow an enemy advance a number of naturally-defined zones were created. These were mainly bounded by water-courses which were strengthened with fixed defences, or planned demolitions. The River Witham runs diagonally across the County from Lincoln to Boston, the line being continued to the Trent at Torksey, by the Foss Dyke. This line could be defended in either direction, depending on whether the threat came from the Grimsby area and the north-east coast, or from the Wash in the south. The Wash threat was further contained by the South Forty-Foot Drain, where defensive features survive. At the A52 crossing of the Drain, is a Type 22 pillbox, and where the railway crosses, the bridge [Bridge No. 18] was mined. This Tunnel for Military Purposes was uncovered and blocked up during a major reconstruction of the bridge in 1988. Explosive would

STICKFORD [Lincs.]. the embrasure with 9-bolt mounting plate for 6 pdr. Hotchkiss QF gun, in a Type 28a emplacement; TF351582.

have been placed under the supporting girders of the bridge in tunnels, deep under the abutments, designed to retain the explosive effect and cause maximum damage. Other bridges in the area were treated in the same way. Near Swineshead Bridge several AT blocks remain by the railway-line, which, here, runs alongside the Drain. Small AT cylinders are found at several points alongside the River Witham near Tattershall Bridge. A more solidly defensive line, parallel to the coast defences, is afforded by the Hobhole Drain, which runs north from the Haven. Until recently, all the crossing-points were defended by pillboxes, [15 seen in 1985], a mixture of Type 22 and Type 23[Lincs.], some of which survive. At the rail-crossing, the existing pillbox was supported by a mass of AT blocks. A further layer was added by pairs of gun-emplacements [Type 28a] built to take 6 pounder Hotchkiss QF guns. These would have swept the flat fields west of the Hobhole Drain, destroying any enemy armour which might have penetrated the line. In the embrasure of each of the four of these which still stand, can be seen the concrete pedestal and its 9-bolt holdfast which would have held the gun.

In the north, three lines were identified as Stop Lines. The New River Ancholme runs due-south, past Brigg, down to a point level with Market Rasen, on whose other side is the end of a line which runs along the River Freshney from west of Grimsby, following other streams past Thorganby, Kirmond-le-Mire, and Ludford. Another line ran from the coast near Donna Nook, following streams and dykes, past North Somercotes and Conisholme, to join the Louth Navigation at High Bridge House, and terminate on the outskirts of the town. Military grid maps of the time, show these last two lines marked in green crayon, but there appears to be no surviving evidence of attempts to improve on natural barriers here.

THE DERBYSHIRE RIVER LINE

Although this line does not figure in contemporary planning, it is clearly visible on the ground. It appears to have its origin where the Coventry Canal crosses the River Tame at Fazeley, south of Tamworth [Staffordshire] and then follows the Tame as far as its confluence with the Trent, on the Derbyshire border south of Burton. There are around 20 pillboxes on this section, plus some more on the Coventry Canal where it forms the northern perimeter defence of RAF Lichfield. The Trent forms the county boundary, up to Newton Solney, where the line branches north up the River Dove to Uttoxeter, still constituting the Derbyshire boundary. From Doveridge, the line continues up the river through Rocester, as far as Ashbourne, where it seems to stop. Along its entire length, the rivers form quite adequate AT barriers, with pillboxes every half-mile [0.8 km.] or so. The majority of the pillboxes, [1 2 out of 17 in the Staffordshire section, and 37 out of 49 on the Derbyshire stretch], are FW3/Type 24 [thin-walled]. This is an hexagonal design with five faces with outwardly-splayed rifle loopholes. The sixth, rear face is longer, and has a centrally-placed doorway, with a pistol-loop either side. The walls are 15-18" thick [35-45 cm.], with a 12" thick [30 cm.] roof-slab. All have had timber shuttering giving them a smooth concrete finish. One, at Ellastone [Derbys.] is built high on a solid, concrete plinth to gain visibility. A solitary Type 23 at the Trent rail crossing

RIVER DOVE LINE [Derbys.]. Rectangular pillbox with sloping roof, a local design confined to this defence line; SKI73298.

ROCESTER [Derbys.]. Thin-walled Type 24 pillbox; SK111398.

HOBHOLE DRAIN [Lincs.]. Type 22 pill-box covering crossing; TF385583.

ELLASTONE [Derbys.]. Emplacement for field-gun disguised as farm building by the addition of a corrugated roof supported on posts; SK120424.

near Alrewas, is treated similarly. Another raill/river crossing nearer to Burton, has four, high-level, two-man pillboxes, on the rail-bridge, above the river. One pillbox type, of which there are six examples extant, appears unique to the area. It is a rectangular design with a loop in each face, an entrance, a large, solid anti-ricochet wall inside, and, its defining feature, a sloping roof. It comes in two sizes- one is 13′ by 1 O′ [4 x 3 m], and the other measures 1 0′6″ by 7′ [3.2 x 2.1 m]. One example, of the larger dimension, stands on a plinth. Another structure on this line is quite unique. It stands at Ellastone [Derbys.] and is a gunhouse, probably for something like a 75mm gun on a wheeled carriage. It is camouflaged to look like a cow-shed, with a gabled roof on concrete posts, which disguises its half-hexagonal front elevation. At the back, the entrance, down steps, is screened by a blast-wall, so the only way of introducing the gun is through the front embrasure. This is the way several 6 pounder Hotchkiss emplacements work, but, here, there seems to be no tell-tale pedestal and holdfast. Under the false gable, is a solid roof, built of railway sleepers. Traces of brown and green camouflage paint may still be seen. At

Mayfield, a large, stone-built pillbox is built into the river-bank. It is half-hexagonal to the front, where six loopholes can cover the river and the bridge. Inside, is a Y-shaped anti-ricochet wall. A passage into the bank is revetted in stone to allow access to the side entrance. It is quite possible that other defence lines existed. By building on the relationship of a pillbox at Shardlow, the AT obstacles on the railway bridge at Melbourne, and two spigot mortar pedestals covering the bridge at Swarkestone, one could argue, quite plausibly, for a line based on the River Trent in Derbyshire. No doubt, local commanders made the best possible use of natural features, and tried to protect key lines of communication. If the result resembled a designated defence line, then that was what it was.

Map to show Coast Batteries

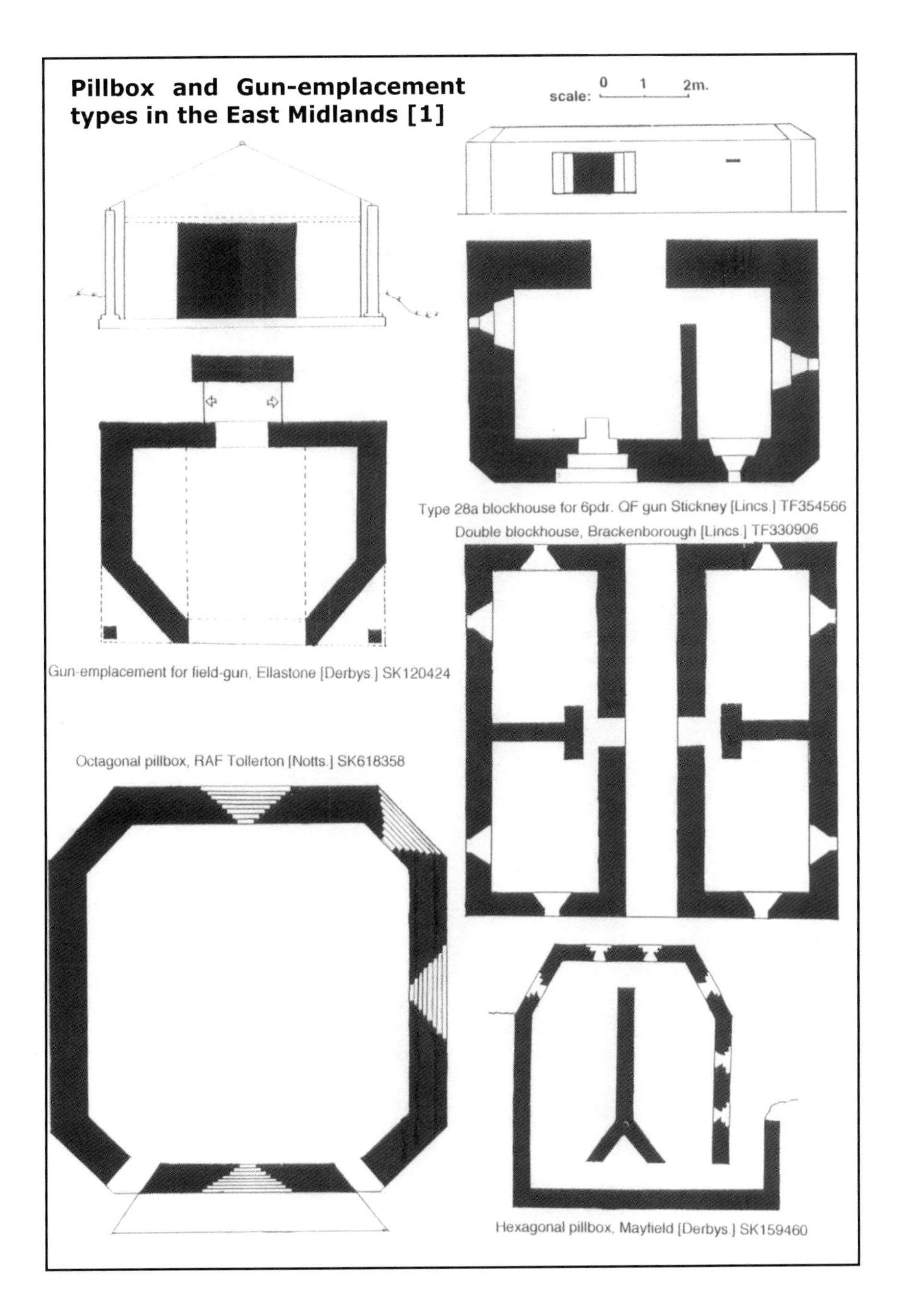
Pillbox and Gun-emplacement types in the East Midlands [1]
scale: 0 1 2m.
Gun-emplacement for field-gun, Ellastone [Derbys.] SK120424
Type 28a blockhouse for 6pdr. QF gun Stickney [Lincs.] TF354566
Double blockhouse, Brackenborough [Lincs.] TF330906
Octagonal pillbox, RAF Tollerton [Notts.] SK618358
Hexagonal pillbox, Mayfield [Derbys.] SK159460

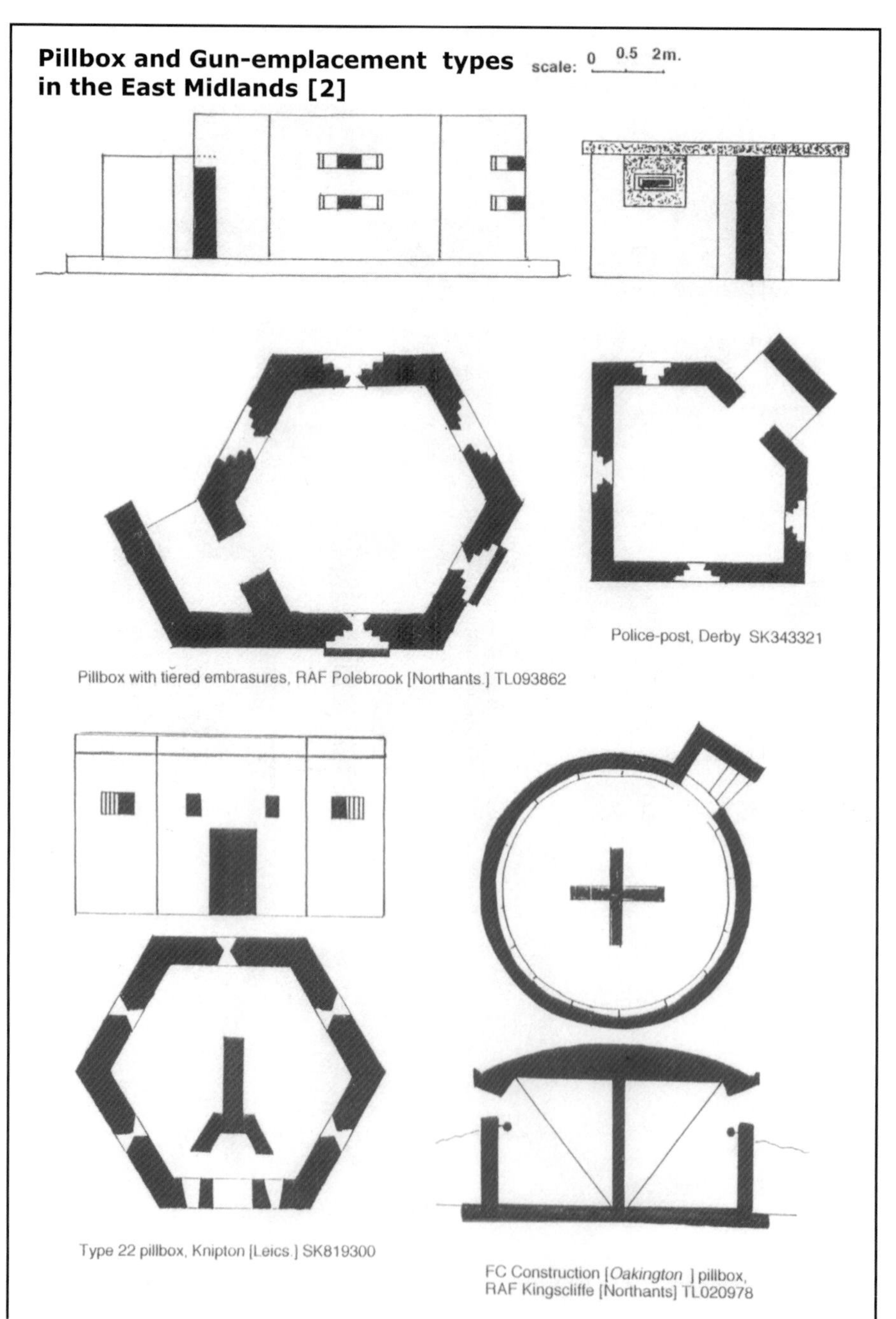

Pillbox with tiered embrasures, RAF Polebrook [Northants.] TL093862

Police-post, Derby SK343321

Type 22 pillbox, Knipton [Leics.] SK819300

FC Construction [*Oakington*] pillbox, RAF Kingscliffe [Northants] TL020978

Pillbox and Gun-emplacement types in the East Midlands [3]

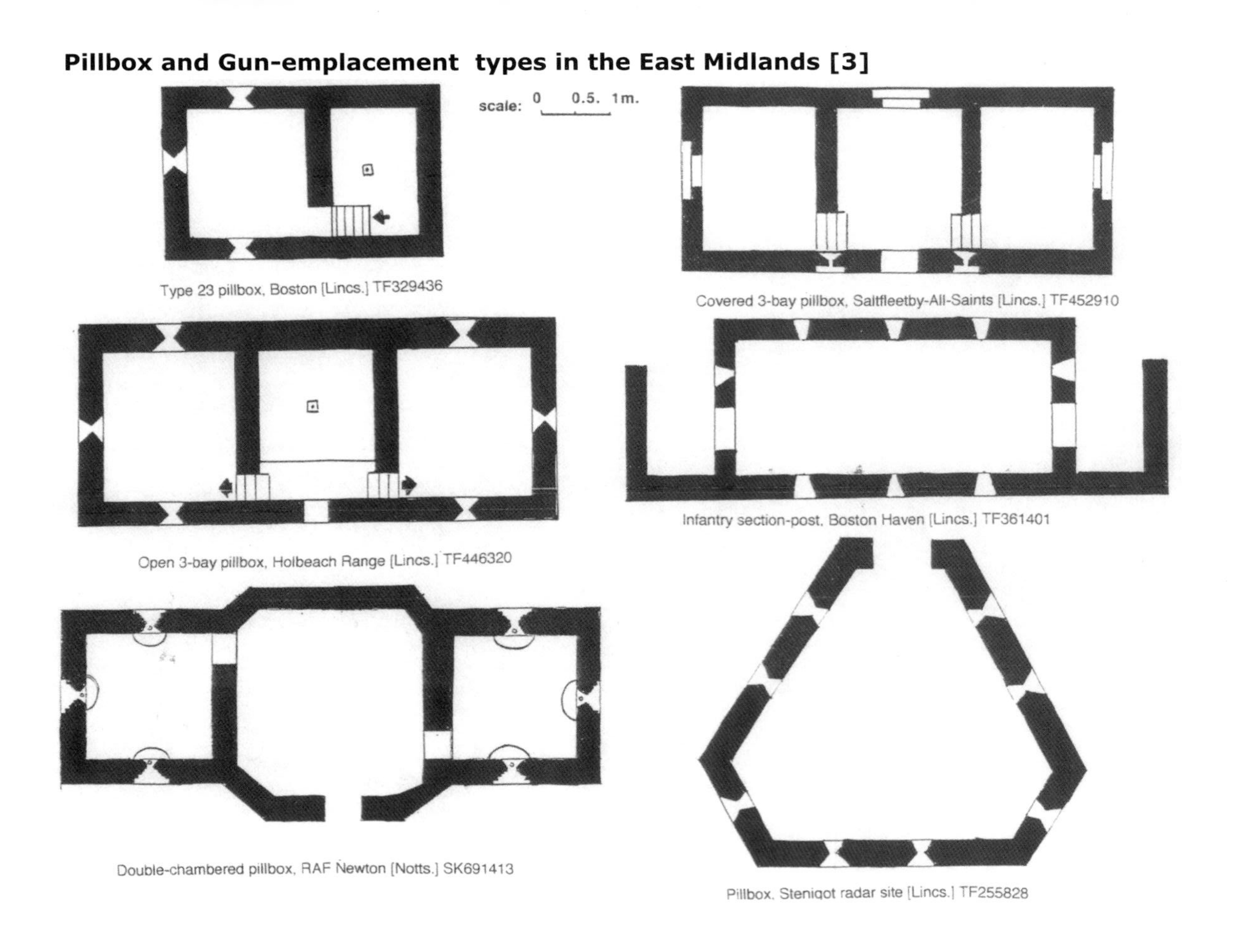

Type 23 pillbox, Boston [Lincs.] TF329436

Covered 3-bay pillbox, Saltfleetby-All-Saints [Lincs.] TF452910

Open 3-bay pillbox, Holbeach Range [Lincs.] TF446320

Infantry section-post, Boston Haven [Lincs.] TF361401

Double-chambered pillbox, RAF Newton [Notts.] SK691413

Pillbox, Steniqot radar site [Lincs.] TF255828

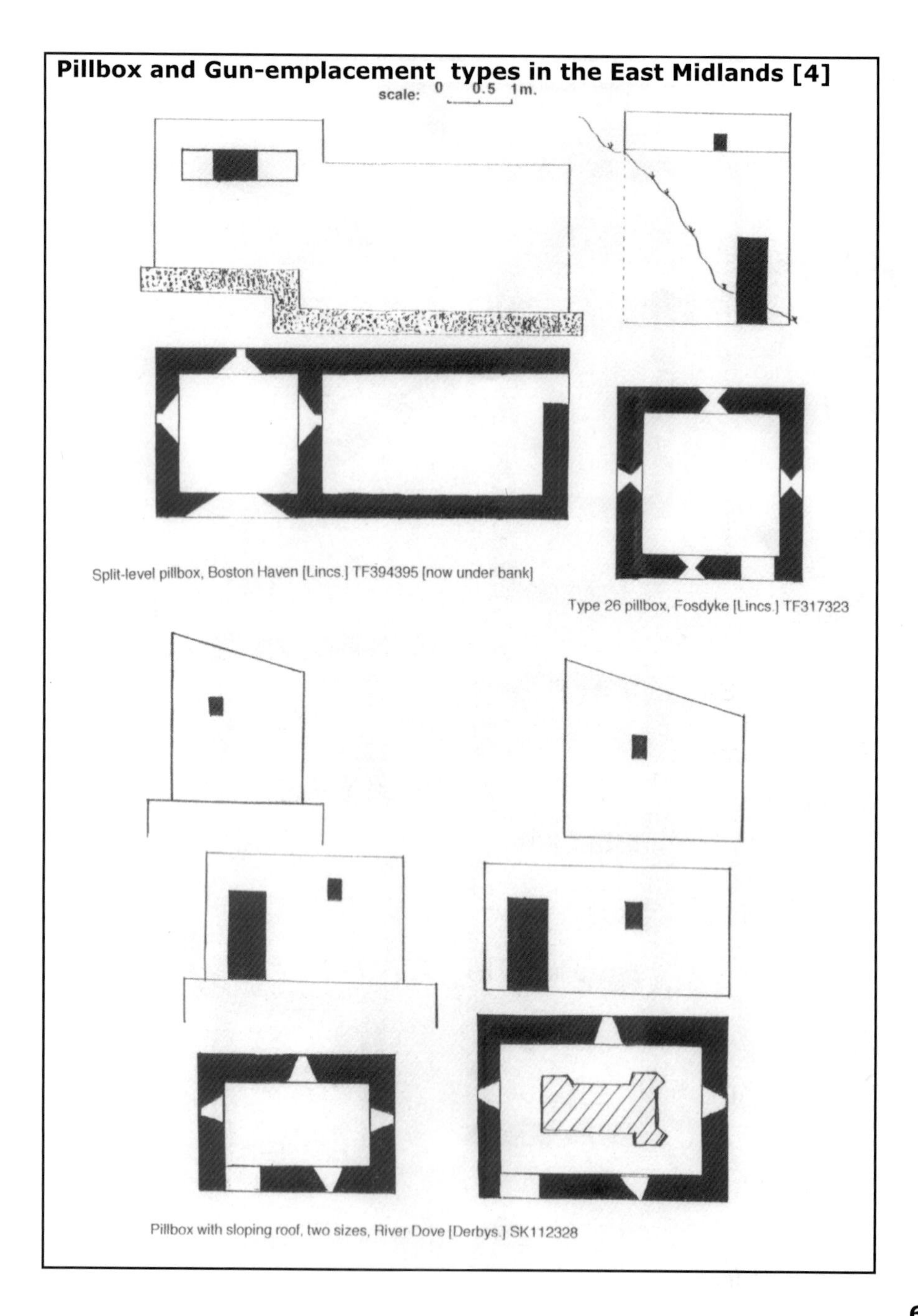

Split-level pillbox, Boston Haven [Lincs.] TF394395 [now under bank]

Type 26 pillbox, Fosdyke [Lincs.] TF317323

Pillbox with sloping roof, two sizes, River Dove [Derbys.] SK112328

4 DEFENCE OF VULNERABLE POINTS

General Ironside's anti-invasion planning, based on fixed fortifications, backed by mobile counter-attacking reserves, was only ever seen as a short-lived strategy born out of necessity. By late autumn 1940, the factories had produced significant numbers of tanks, trucks and artillery, and a great deal of training of troops had taken place. Ironside had decreed that, even at the height of pillbox construction, troops were to spend no more than a quarter of their time on it- they must train. His successor, General Brooke [later Lord Alanbrooke], was able to put a stop on the building of fixed linear defences, and focus on mobility, based on defended nodal points. From now on, key places on roads, railways and waterways were to receive all-round defences

SHORTS CORNER [Lincs.]: Rectangular pillbox, Type 23 Lincolnshire version, modified for infantry use, by roofing over the central well; TF312529.

HOSE LODGE FARM [Notts.]. Type 22 pillbox protecting a searchlight site. This local pattern has two pistol-loops flanking the door; SK718308.

based on the notion of defending points not lines, and of thus controlling access, not of holding territory. Thus the River Trent, downstream from Newark moved from being a barrier held in strength along its length, to being a sequence of points needing to be secured against enemy airborne landing. By the summer of 1941, Memoranda issued by Trentforce, from its HQ at 31 Derby Road, Nottingham, detailed the precise responsibilities of the available forces.The Trent River Patrol, a force of some 500 men with rifles, light machine-guns, and 30 patrol boats, was charged with holding the locks and bridges all along the river, from Gunthorpe, through Newark, Cromwell Lock, Torksey, Gainsborough, to Keadby. The regular troops of Trentforce permanently manned the defences of key points such as Gainsborough. This perfectly illustrates the sharing of internal security duties between the regular troops of Trentforce, and those of the Home Guard, here represented by the River Patrol. Observation Posts [OPs] were established in church-towers and other vantage points. Motorcycle patrols were detailed to provide messaging services, wireless sets were provided, and the Post Offices at Bingham, Lowdham, Radcliffe, Gunthorpe, Woodborough, and Bridgford [Notts.] were designated Centres of Communication held and worked by armed PO personnel, mobilised as the Post Office Rifles.

ANTI-TANK ISLANDS

Most large towns, and many smaller ones, in our region were designated nodal points, or AT Islands and given all-round defences. These include the following:

Derbyshire: Derby, Chesterfield.
Leicestershire: Leicester.
Lincolnshire: Lincoln, Grantham, Caistor, Horncastle, Boston, Gainsborough.
Northamptonshire: Northampton, Kettering, Wellingborough, Oundle.
Nottinghamshire: Nottingham, Mansfield, Newark, Retford, Worksop.
Rutland: Oakham, Uppingham.

These defences consisted, for the most part of, roadblocks, loopholed walls, AT walls, wire entanglements, and weapons pits. The surviving defence plans, usually from 1941 or 1942, when the threat of invasion had receded, and the defences were almost unnecessary, show a web of Defended Localities [DL] based mainly on roadblocks. Areas, for which specific Home Guard companies were responsible, are generally shown, with details of the Keep, named for the mediaeval notion of a strongpoint held to the death. The DL was often sketched out in some detail to include the manpower and weapons available, and the objectives of the defenders

Derby was ringed by around 20 roadblocks roughly located where each main road crossed the Borough boundary. Many of these were also the centres of DLs. Other DLs were located on specific buildings such as Normanton Barracks, and the Derby Cables works on the Alfreton Road. Railblocks were also employed, with one covering the LMS main line between Spondon Station and the lines into the LMS Works, and Nottingham Road Station. The HQ of the defences appears to have been at the Becket Street drill hall. The city was defended by 13 and 14 Bns. of the Derbyshire

SINFIN [Derbys.]. Police-post guarding factory; SK342322.

Home Guard, with a demarcation line running north to south from the A608, north of the Racecourse, down through the Market Place, Babington Lane, and Normanton Road, past the Barracks, and then along the railway line south-east by the Qualcast works, and through Osmaston.

Northampton was circled by two concentric rings of roadblocks, the inner following the Borough boundary, and the outer thrown out along the main routes into town. There were also four railblocks at Hardingstone junction, Kingsthorpe railway bridge, Duston junction, and near St John's Street station. The Keep, the final centre of resistance, was split into three locations- the Clare Street drill hall, which was the Home Guard HQ; the police station in The Mounts; and the old regimental depot of the Northamptonshires in Barrack Road. The defence of the town was the responsibility of the 12 Bn. Northants. Home Guard, which had absorbed the early LDV companies, and those based on works, such as the Express Lifts, Electric Light, Gas, and Railway Coys. As tactics were modified, the system of Defended Localities was adopted, and some of the former roadblocks were developed to meet this new demand.

STAPLEFORD [Notts.], Ruck pillbox, common in the north-east, but very unusual further south. This is the only known example; SK478378.

The material on Leicester is far patchier, but, it would appear from the available evidence, that a perimeter, similar to those of Northampton and Derby, was drawn around the city, and defended by roadblocks. What is clear in Leicestershire, is the network of LDV posts, later manned every night by the Home Guard, which existed in the hinterland around the city, a sort of invasion early-warning system. This parallels the Northampton experience, where posts, with and without shelter, are listed. These are not to be confused with Observer Corps posts [see Chapter 6].

Wellingborough's Keep was an area, in the town centre bounded by High Street, Salem Lane, Herriott's Lane, Great Park Road, Market Street, and Silver Street. This was completely surrounded by wire entanglements, chain mines, bent-rail roadblocks, with each junction or weak point covered by Spigot Mortars, Northover Projectors, or light machine-guns. In March 1942, the garrison of the Keep was five officers and 175 other ranks of B Coy. 7th Northants Bn. Home Guard, armed with personal weapons plus four Spigot Mortars, five Northover Projectors, three light machine-guns [Brens by this date, but earlier they would have been Lewis], and six Tommy Guns for house-to-house fighting. HQ was in the Sun Inn, Church Street. As we have seen elsewhere, Defended Localities ringed the town. One was located at the junction of Finedon Road [A510] and Eastfield Road [B573]. Here, with its HQ at No. 10 Eastfield Road, and a reserve HQ opposite at No. 7a, E Coy. held positions around this T-junction by surrounding the whole area with wire, mining the road approaches, and covering possible enemy lines of attack with three Spigot Mortars, four Northover Projectors, and five light machine-guns. At the same time, A Coy. manned a DL at Broad Green, and G Coy. another at Great Harrowden.

The urban settings mean that most of this was swept away even before the end of the War, but certainly, soon after. The AT blocks on Trent Bridge, Nottingham, for instance, were demolished in 1945 in order to restore traffic flow. Remarkably, odd vestiges remain. Pillboxes can be seen at Northampton and Boston; there are spigot-mortar pedestals at Oundle and Oakham; there are AT walls [in Mill Road], sockets for AT rails [on Nettleham Road] and AT cylinders [off Carholme Road], in Lincoln, there is a loop-holed wall in Northampton; in Grantham, AT blocks remain under the railway bridge in Dysart Road, and on the railway embankment on Springfield Road. Most of the pillboxes were standard Type 22, but by the old power-station, alongside the River Nene, in Northampton, there are two quite unusual, circular, open-topped structures, a little like Norcon pillboxes but with a different, stepped profile. The extent of the AT obstacles is shown by the sheer numbers involved - Northampton was defended by over 750 concrete AT blocks.

Villages also received defences. The anti-invasion plans for Lincolnshire included the construction of fortifications in over 30 villages and small towns. Pillboxes remain at Halton Holegate, Horncastle, Spalding and Spilsby, and a spigot mortar pedestal in Stamford. Located astride the crossroads of the old A16 and A17 roads, Sutterton was clearly important as a nodal point. Three of the five pillboxes built to cover road-

OAKHAM [Rutland]. Spigot mortar pedestal on the angle of the castle earthworks; this would, originally, have been set in a pit; SK863090.

blocks still stand [two Type 23 Lincs. and a Type 22] as does a solid, surface air-raid shelter, perhaps doubling as an ammunition store. At Fosdyke, one of its four pillboxes survives. Outside Uffington, is an AT block, and AT cylinders can be seen at Leadenham. In Leicestershire, the 18th Century lock-up in the centre of Worthington village, appears to have had a loophole inserted, and at Gaddesby is a spigot mortar pedestal. Burgh-le-Marsh [Lincs.] formerly had concrete roadblocks with sockets for horizontal RSJs, all controlled by the OP in the fish-and-chip shop. The approach to the village of Great Addington [Northants.] is covered by a loopholed wall. By 1941, all such places had fully-developed Defence Plans which detailed the command structure; the forces available with their weapons and transport; priorities for defence, and procedures for closing roadblocks, carrying out demolitions, demobilising vehicles and destroying supplies to deny them to the enemy. As we have already seen, these usually defined roles for both regular troops and the Home Guard.

SUTTON-ST-EDMUNDS [Lincs.]. Lincolnshire pattern home guard store/shelter, this one on a Searchlight site; TF367118.

A remarkable set of Home Guard defence plans survives in the Nottinghamshire Archive collection. The defences of the centre of Newark, and DLs in its outskirts and surrounding villages are shown in great detail. Weaponry is restricted to rifles, a few Lewis guns, Northover Projectors and Thompson sub-machine guns, but clever use is made of local knowledge in the siting of road-blocks covered by bombing parties, and in the choice of location for the Lewis guns, giving them the optimum field of fire. Detail extends to the numbers of troops available, the locations of wire barriers, trenches and 0Ps. As well as Newark's immediate hinterland, which is illustrated here, a number of more distant villages such as Colston Bassett, Eakring, Lockwell and Thurgarton [Notts.) are also depicted. Each is defended by a platoon of Home Guardsmen ranging from a strength of 24 at Hickling to 42 at Farnsfield. The total strength of the Newark force was 341 rifles, plus 12 Lewis Guns, five Tommy-guns and a Northover Projector. Added to this would have been the ground defence force of RAF Winthorpe, probably with improvised armoured vehicles, the Trent River Patrol, and numbers of regular troops stationed in the area.

OTHER VULNERABLE POINTS

Important road junctions were often defended. Examples include a pillbox on a T-junction near Underwood [Notts.], a spigot mortar pedestal and Home Guard store on the A607 at Rotherby [Leics.], two prefabricated, square pillboxes by the A46 at Ratcliffe-on-Wreake [Leics.], and a pillbox [type 23 Lincs. for infantry] at Frithville. At Pode Hole [Lincs.] was a Type 23 [Lincs.] pillbox and AT blocks. At Stapleford [Notts.] is a loopholed Stanton shelter, similar to the Ruck Pillbox built in great numbers in the north-eastern counties.

The important Chain-Home Radar site at Stenigot, was defended by pillboxes of unusual design. Triangular, with chamfered corners, large enough to contain loopholes, they are, in effect, hexagonal. In one, the entrance is in one of the long sides. On the roof is a hexagonal position for a LAA gun. The only similar pillbox to this, is at another radar site at Ventnor, on the Isle of Wight. At Firestone Hill [Derbys.], a radio station is defended by two standard Type 22 pillboxes, placed back-to-back on the narrow spine of the hill, commanding both approaches.

A number of HQs were defended such as Nottingham Castle, with a rectangular blockhouse inside the castle gate, and Louth Park Farm [Lincs.] [see Chapter 6] Brackenborough Hall [Lincs.], requisitioned by Northern Command in 1940, was HQ for the anti-invasion forces around Louth. The site was fortified with weapons pits, covered with corrugated sheeting and made to look like compost heaps and suchlike. In the farm-yard are two brick and concrete blockhouses. One is rectangular, divided into two compartments, each with two loopholes. Two more of these modules are linked under one roof to form a square, double blockhouse with central corridor, and four compartments with a total of eight loopholes. At Launde Abbey [Leics.] a string of 44 AT cylinders line the drive.

Other Vulnerable Points which received pillbox protection were Searchlight Sites [see Chapter 6], airfields [see Chapter 5], and factories. There is a loopholed defence post at the entrance to a former factory site in Derby, and combination fire-watching/defence posts, similar to Naval police-posts, survive on the roofs of factories in Great Billing, and Balmoral Road, Kingsthorpe [Northants.]. A recent TV report featured such a post on the roof of Newton's factory in Alfreton Road, Derby.

THE HOME GUARD

As the responsibility for repelling possible coastal or airborne raids devolved onto the Home Guard, it was realised that they needed a little more muscle than that afforded by rifles and Lewis guns. There evolved a range of weapons known officially as sub-artillery. There were several examples in general use. The Northover Projector, a sort of drainpipe on legs, fired Molotov Cocktails or phosphorus grenades. The Spigot Mortar or Blacker Bombard fired a 141b. anti-personnel bomb or a 20lb. AT bomb from a mortar mounted either on a field tripod with spade feet, or from a perma-

OUNDLE [Northants.]. Twin home guard store/shelters behind the Drill Hall. One is for explosives and the other for inflammables, one has had steel doors fitted, and this may have been to enable the storage of a Smith gun; TLO34883.

nent pedestal. This pedestal, about 3' [0.9m] high, like a concrete oil-drum, had a stainless steel pintle attached to a steel framework embedded in the concrete. It stood in a pit lined with built-in brick ammunition lockers. The mortar would be kept safe, and only brought out and mounted immediately prior to action. It had an effective range of about 100 yards/metres. Over time, the pit has generally filled up, and, often, all that is visible is a shiny, stainless steel pin in a grass verge. Examples remain all over the region, the most obvious, probably being that on the castle earthworks at Oakham. The other, fairly common piece of sub-artillery was the Smith gun. This 3" smooth-bore gun came with disc wheels and limber. It was designed to be towed into action by an Austin Seven-sized car, or even manhandled. The gun was then turned on its side, one wheel functioning as a turntable. It fired an AT round, and its range was 200 yards/metres, but the hand-book recommends 100 yards/metres as the realistic range for moving targets.

NORTHAMPTON, unusual, circular, open pillbox probably based on the Norcon sewer-pipe design. One of two guarding the Power Station; SP766596.

These Home Guard weapons needed to be stored somewhere securely. The rules laid down separate stores for inflammables and explosives. The most common store in the Eastern counties is rectangular, brick-built with a concrete slab root, the size of a lock-up garage. It has a door in the middle of a long side or at one end, and one or two ventilation holes, high up in the end walls. Stores like this can be seen at Nassington [Northants.]. Behind Oundle Drill Hall [Northants.], the town's HQ in the event of attack, is a pair of such stores. One has had its front door replaced by a pair of steel doors. This could have been done to accommodate a Smith Gun. So long as there was a brick dividing wall, then only one, dual-purpose Store was necessary. This meant that Nissen huts were used as stores as well as the purpose-built ones. In Lincolnshire, a Store with a shallow, gabled roof, and the door in the middle of a long side, was adopted. Examples of these survive at Auborn, at Louth and Winterton [both associated with ROC posts], and Sutton-St-Edmund, on a Searchlight Site. A third, L-shaped, design survives in the churchyard at Humberston. Other ad-hoc buildings also seem to have been used, as at Tattershall [Lincs.], where the Store has a more steeply-gabled roof, than was usual, and low, exterior blast-walls. Many Home Guard units were recruited in the work-place, and had their base there. Express Lifts in Northampton is a good example. One other example of Home Guard structure deserves a mention. The Auxiliary Units were self-contained cells of guerrillas who would fight on after an invasion, from behind enemy lines. They operated out of Operational Bases, sunken huts with secret entrances and exits, equipped with food and weapons. These dotted the countryside of coastal areas, and, for security reasons were frequently re-located. A recent archaeological survey of Brocklesby revealed six such sites in quite a small area. The HQ and training centre for the Lincolnshire Auxiliary Units was Dalby Hall.

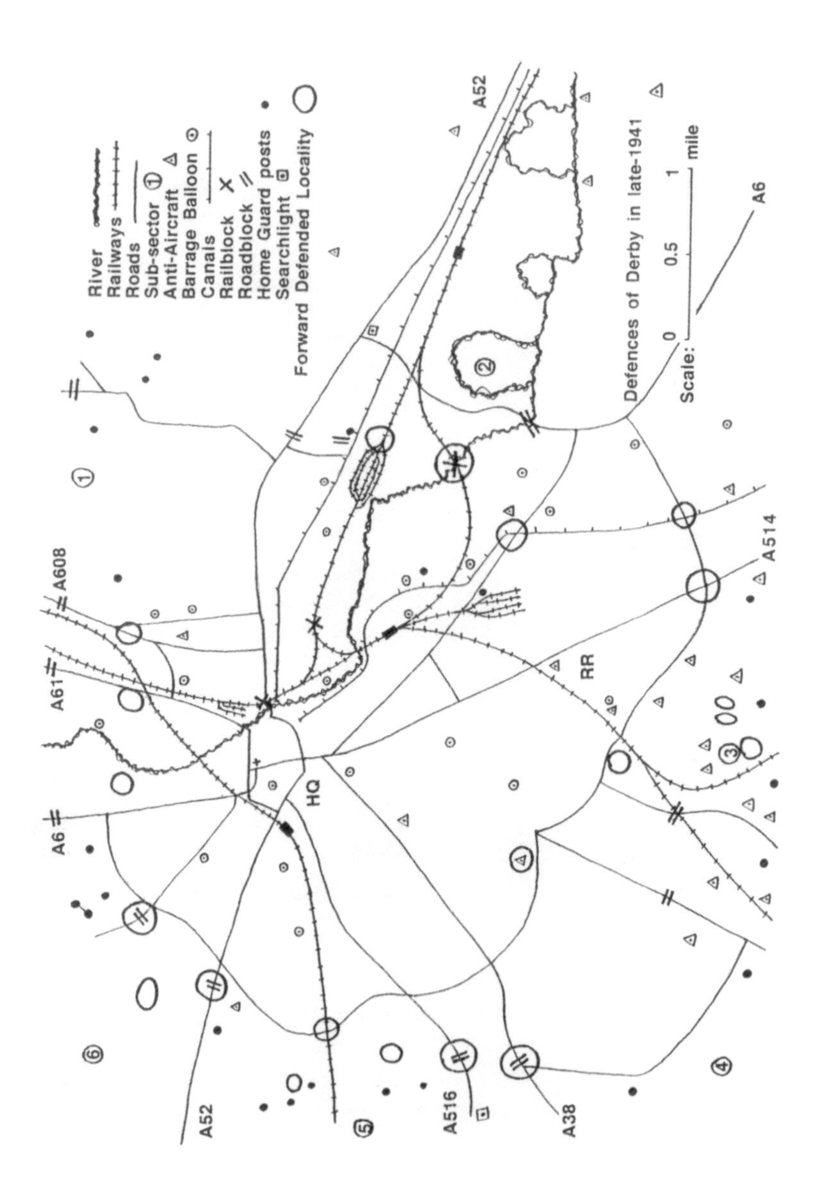

Defences of Derby in late-1941

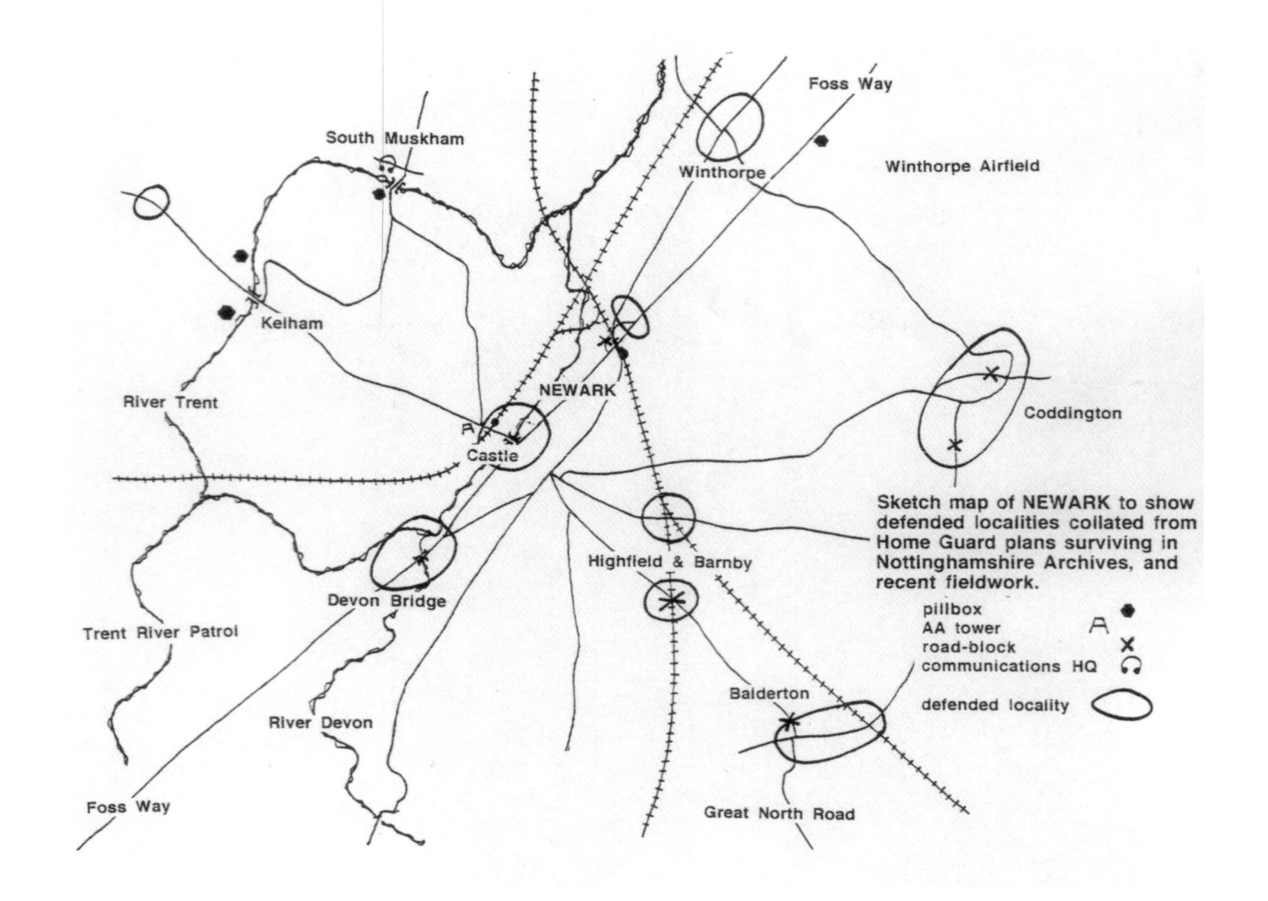
South Muskham
Foss Way
Winthorpe
Winthorpe Airfield
Kelham
NEWARK
River Trent
Castle
Coddington
Sketch map of NEWARK to show defended localities collated from Home Guard plans surviving in Nottinghamshire Archives, and recent fieldwork.
Highfield & Barnby
Devon Bridge
pillbox
AA tower
road-block
communications HQ
Trent River Patrol
Balderton
defended locality
River Devon
Foss Way
Great North Road

5 AIRFIELD DEFENCES

First World War airfields were guarded, but as no concerted attack from the air or on the ground was realistically anticipated, no fixed defences were provided. In 1940, airfields were perceived as being no more vulnerable than other military installations. However, even though the threat of invasion had faded by early-1941, the German airborne attack on Crete, targeting airfields, highlighted the potential threat of such raids. Consequently, airfields continued to be given fixed defences, even after such provision elsewhere, had generally ceased. The Air Ministry, through the Taylor Report, issued late-September 1940, assigned airfields to categories of risk. Those near ports, or close to selected vulnerable points or Aircraft Storage Units, Class I airfields, were to be provided with the most fixed defences. Those likely to be involved in counter-attacking an enemy force, Class II airfields, were deemed to need less heavy defences. All the rest, Class III, received less. In our region, most of the Lincolnshire airfields in existence by late 1940, were categorised as Class I, with some in Class II. There were also a number of other Class II airfields - Balderton, Hucknall, Newton, Syerston, Tollerton and Winthorpe [Notts.]. Bitteswell, Bottesford, and Saltby [Leics.]. Cottesmore, North Luffenham and Woolfox Lodge [Rutland]; Chipping Warden, Hinton-in-the-Hedges, Kingscliffe and Polebrook [Northants.], and Burnaston [Derby.]. Class I airfields were expected to have up to 30 or more pillboxes, in concentric rings facing inward over the landing area, and out, to the field. For Class II, this was cut to around 20 pillboxes. Added to these were the disappearing pillboxes known as Pickett-Hamilton Forts, dummy pillboxes, rifle-pits, armoured vehicles, and LAA defences which could be dual-purpose; altogether some formidable fortifications. Early in the War, defences were manned by regular troops, supplemented by

MARKET HARBOROUGH [Leics.]. Standard Battle HQ; SP718895.

details of airmen. By 1942, the RAF Regiment had been formed, specifically for the defence of airfields against air and ground attack.

Given these designated levels of provision, it is quite remarkable how little can be seen on the ground. Either, there were concerted programmes of demolition at the end of the War, or pillboxes were never built in the numbers envisaged by Taylor. There are heavily-fortified airfields such as Tollerton [Notts.], Wellingore [Lincs.] and Kingscliffe [Northants.], all in Class II, but equally, there are airfields such as Hemswell and Kirton-in-Lindsey [Lincs.], both in Class I, where no defence structures of any sort are visible, although both are recorded as being beneficiaries of Pickett Hamilton forts. At some USAAF airfields, the defence was mobile, relying on 0.5″ heavy machine-guns mounted on trucks, but, there again, some of their airfields were given fixed defences by the new tenants. There are an awful lot of inconsistencies around airfield defences.

HUCKNALL [Notts.]. Unique Battle HQ to local design; SK519475.

AIRFIELD DEFENCE STRUCTURES

Pillboxes are the most common defence structures to be found on our airfields, but they include a wide variety of types. The Type 22 is found at Barkston Heath, Digby, Coleby

Grange, and Wellingore [Lincs.]. These were, likely, all built early in the War, and at Wellingore, are fitted with mountings, semi-circular toothed rings, probably Scarff mountings for Lewis guns, and, by the look of them, come straight out of World War I aircraft.

There are larger, hexagonal pillboxes with 42" [1.1 m] thick walls, and fewer than six loops, at Sywell [Northants.], Hucknall and Newton [Notts.], Binbrook and Grantham [Lincs.]. These could be Air Ministry designs from early 1941. Later that year, a directive went out to thicken walls, and reduce the number of loopholes. At Sywell and Grantham the anti-ricochet walls are tri-leafed, and sprung from the floor. At all of them, the entrances are through some sort of low porch, or tunnel with a loophole above. There are eight examples at Tollerton [Notts.] of a different hexagonal design with five loopholes for Turnbull mounts for light machine-guns, and one pistol loop by the entrance. Another, different, hexagonal design can be seen at Polebrook [Northants]. Here, in one pillbox, two adjacent faces, and in another, two alternate faces have two loops, one above the other. There is no obvious explanation for this. At Tollerton and Newton [Notts.] are several examples of a design not found anywhere else in Britain. A large, square pillbox, has chamfered corners, large enough to accommodate a loophole, hence producing an irregular octagon. Nine survive at Tollerton, and two at Newton. These all have Turnbull mounts, and, interestingly, each pillbox has no more than five loops in its eight faces. Also at Newton is the Air Ministry equivalent of the Type FWD3/23 [Lincs.] with two, square, loopholed chambers, linked by an open LAA position. This example is unique to Britain, but one in Northern Ireland may be the same. At Cottesmore [Leics.] there are two odd structures at Warren Farm. One is a half-hexagonal pillbox built onto the end of a farm building. The other is a hexagonal pillbox with an open annexe containing the mounting for a LAA machine-gun. It is tempting to regard a hexagonal pillbox at Hinton-in-the-Hedges, surmounted by a gazebo-like structure as an example of camouflage. The explanation is sadly prosaic, however, as the superstructure represents the airfield's Homer Beacon. At North Coates [Lincs.], there are at least three Type 23 [Lincs.] pillboxes built into the Sea Bank, which here doubles as airfield perimeter, and coast defence position.

A quite distinct, mushroom-shaped, circular pillbox, to Drawing No. 9882/41 by the FC Construction Company, but more often described on official airfield plans as Oakinqton or Fairlop pillboxes, is plentiful in our region. They were designed to give all-round fields of fire, and are sometimes found in mutually supporting pairs, often linked by communications trenches. There were originally 11 at Burnaston [Derbys.] but all have now been demolished. They survive, however, at Chipping Warden, Croughton, Hinton-in-the-Hedges, Grafton Underwood and Kingscliffe [Northants.]. The Kingscliffe airfield plan records these pillboxes as "Mushroom" to Drawing No.TG/14.

Found in conjunction with the FC Construction pillboxes at Croughton and Hinton-in-the-Hedges are Seaqull Trenches. So called from their M-shaped outline from the air, these are brick-lined trenches, with concrete, overhead cover, usually

KINGSCLIFFE [Northants.]. FC Construction or Oakington pillbox, one of four on this airfield, sited in pairs as strongpoints; TLO26972.

KINGSCLIFFE [Northants.]. Loopholed fighter dispersal pen. Similar pens can be seen at Wellingore & Coleby Grange [Lincs.], Culmhead [Somerset], and at Drem [Lothian]; TLO21979.

mounded with earth. Turnbull mounts are built into the firing observation slits.

At a number of fighter stations, the dispersal pens, around the edge of the airfield, were fortified. The E-shaped earth traverses were raised over brick-built shelters for air-crew and ground staff, and their outer walls were loopholed for close defence, an arrangement resembling the Carnot walls in the dry moats of Victorian forts. This arrangement can be seen particularly well at Kingscliffe [Northants.] and Coleby Grange and Wellingore [Lincs.].

The Pickett-Hamilton fort was a retractable gunpost worked by compressed air. They were installed, in threes, on large numbers of airfields in late-1940 and early- 1941. Fourteen airfields in Lincolnshire were provided with them. The fort consisted of a cylindrical, loopholed chamber, entered from above, through a hatch. This was sunk into the ground, inside a concrete sleeve, flush with the ground, near the grass landing strip. If enemy aircraft attempted to land,

POLEBROOK [Northants.]. One of two such pillboxes with twin loops in adjacent faces in one pillbox, and alternate faces in the other; TL093862.

then the fort would be raised pneumatically, and the two men inside could fire on them. This concept was embraced enthusiastically by Churchill, who ordered their proliferation, despite the impractical realities of their use.

Airfields were liberally provided with LAA guns, often in sandbagged pits, but sometimes in more substantial constructions. At East Kirkby [Lincs.] a Hispano-Suiza gun has been re-mounted in a reconstructed position, whilst others ring the airfield. At Kingscliffe, several LAA positions of a different style remain. These are paired sewer-pipes, in figure-of-eight conformation, one of each pair containing the fitting for a Stork mounting to carry twin Lewis or Vickers machine-guns, or, with minor modifications, Brownings. A pit fitted for a Stork mounting survives at Sywell. The Air Ministry handbook for this mounting is dated January 1943. Before that, mountings appear to have been of the post type, as survives at Cottesmore, or in the Type 23 and Type 23 [Lincs.] pillboxes. Some of the surface 50-man air-raid shelters at Kingscliffe, have been strengthened with con-

TOLLERTON [Notts.]. Octagonal pillbox, one of nine at this heavily- defended training airfield; there are two similar pillboxes at Newton [Notts.]; each pillbox has loopholes in only four or five faces; SK618358.

crete girdles, to enable LAA positions to be erected on their roofs.

The defence of the airfield was directed from the Battle HQ [BHQ]. This was usually built to Drawing No.1 1008/41, and consisted of a sunken chamber containing office and communications centre etc. with a raised concrete observation cupola at one end giving all-round visibility. It had two entrances, one through a hatch beside the cupola, and the other up steps from a door below ground level. Examples can be seen at Bruntingthorpe and Market Harborough [Leics.], North Luffenham [Rutland], Ossington [Notts.], Grafton Underwood, Hinton-in-the-Hedges, Kingscliffe and Polebrook [Northants.]. Binbrook, Grantham, Hibaldstow, Swinderby, Wellingore and Wickenby [Lincs.]. There are also examples of non-standard Battle HQs. Hucknall has a three-storey tower, Drawing No.TG1, described as the Battle HQ on the airfield plan. At Chipping Warden [Northants.], Adrian Armishaw has identified a sunken, L-shaped structure made up of buried Stanton shelters as a possible Battle HQ. When

GOXHILL [Lincs.]. Standard Battle HQ with specially elevated cupola to give a more effective command of the airfield; TA108207.

the USAAF moved into Goxhill [Lincs.], they found that the existing Battle HQ [11008/41] did not give them sufficient visibility, so they added another storey onto the cupola. What is strange at Goxhill, is that there are two more standard Battle HQ cupolas on the perimeter of the airfield, with Stanton shelters tacked onto their ends, and labelled as Observation Posts. At Sywell [Northants], the Battle HQ was built into a stone barn, with loopholed gables, only recently destroyed. It has been suggested that the PBX [Telephone Exchange], at Kingscliffe, to Drawing No.5648/41, is a conversion of an earlier type of Battle HQ to Drawing No.3329/41.

It is worth noting that the late 20th Century quardpost used to guard operational airfields, and referred to as a sangar, is very little different from the Norcon pillboxes of World War II.

GOXHILL [Lincs.]. One of two structures identified on the Air Ministry plan of the airfield as Observation Posts, consisting of a Stanton shelter with a standard Battle HQ cupola tacked on the end; TA 113223.

APPROACHES TO AIRFIELD DEFENCE

The earliest approach was to defend the perimeter- A string of pillboxes was built around the edge of the airfield, supplemented by wire, trenches, weapon pits etc. This is well seen at Wellingore, where at least seven Type 22 pillboxes, a BHQ, and six loopholed aircraft dispersal pens, completely ring the airfield with defences. Tollerton [Notts.] is even more heavily-defended. An unbroken ring of 19 pillboxes, alternately hexagonal and octagonal, protects this airfield. There is even a pillbox built inside one of the hangars used by MAP, with three loops facing only the interior. As described above, the octagonal pillboxes have loops on only selected sides, but these cover both the landing ground, inwards, and the field, outwards.

By early 1942, the tactics for airfield defence were changing. Gone was the thin, easily breached perimeter, and in its place, was a network of 'defended localities' acting as bases

NORTH LUFFENHAM [Rutland]. Pillbox raised on stilts attached to the 25 yard small-arms range; SK934046.

CONINGSBY [Lincs.]. 1980s sangar on airfield perimeter; TF220570.

for counter-attack, more than ways of holding ground. It is possible that this transition can be seen at Kingscliffe, where two groups of concentrated defences may be discerned, each containing two mushroom pillboxes, and one the BHQ as well. It is almost certain that this is what is visible at Hinton-in-the-Hedges, and at Croughton. Here, are almost islands of defences, at the former, the BHO, two mushroom pillboxes, and three seaqull trenches, and at the latter, a mushroom pillbox and two seaqull trenches. This combination, incidentally, is seen on other, similar airfield defence sites outside our region. Burnaston's defences of BHQ and 11 mushroom pillboxes, seem, however, to be rooted in the earlier perimeter style. In relation to all airfield defences, Colin Dobinson comments that everything; ideas, structures, tactics, weapons etc. was introduced about a year after the need for it had passed.

THE DEFENCES OF SYWELL AERODROME, NORTHAMPTONSHIRE

The first defensive works were constructed at Sywell aerodrome at the beginning of WWII when it became home to 6 Elementary Flying Training School (EFTS) operated by Brooklands Aviation Ltd. providing basic flying training in Tiger Moths. Brooklands also repaired and overhauled 1841 Wellington bombers and Armstrong Whitworth assembled around 100 Lancaster Mk II bombers. Seven pillboxes were built around the perimeter to cover the aerodrome, and also four roadblocks sited on adjacent roads. The pillboxes were Type 22 hexagonal brick structures with reinforced concrete roofs. In the event of an attack, airfield defence would have been co-ordinated from the Battle Headquarters, usually located in a purpose-built underground bunker with a position for viewing the airfield. Sywell's Battle HQ was built inside a derelict stone barn sited on high ground to the east of the aerodrome in order to camouflage it. The aerodrome

Sywell Battle Headquarters

was defended by E Coy 9th (Brixworth) Battalion of the Northamptonshire Home Guard and a 19′ x 32′ brick shed is identified as a store building for their Smith gun. A large hexagonal pillbox with 42″ thick walls and only three loopholes stands on the western side of the aerodrome, suggesting that it was constructed after the perimeter defences, possibly to an Air Ministry design. It has an unusual anti-ricochet wall, the edges of which slope outwards at 60′ from floor to ceiling and a low, dog-legged entrance tunnel. The airfield site plan identifies four anti-aircraft posts around south-east corner of the aerodrome, although when they were recorded on the plan, only the bases remained and no indication is given of the weapons used. A circular sunken brick gun pit survives in good condition near Wood Lodge Farm, and contains the socket for a Stork gun mount. The Stork used a system of springs to counterbalance twin light machine guns mounted on a horizontal arm, which also allowed the guns to engage ground targets.

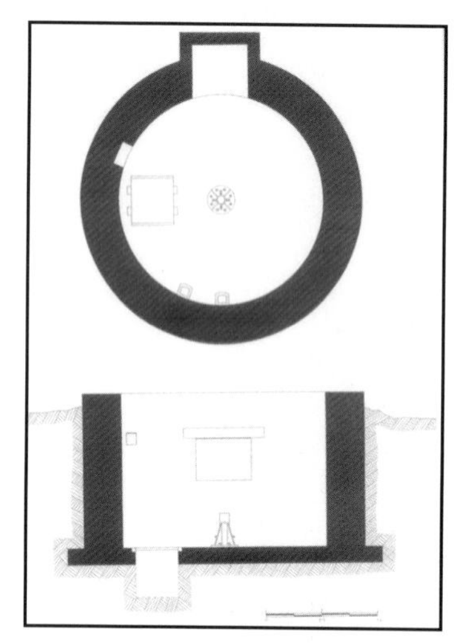

LAA gun-pit

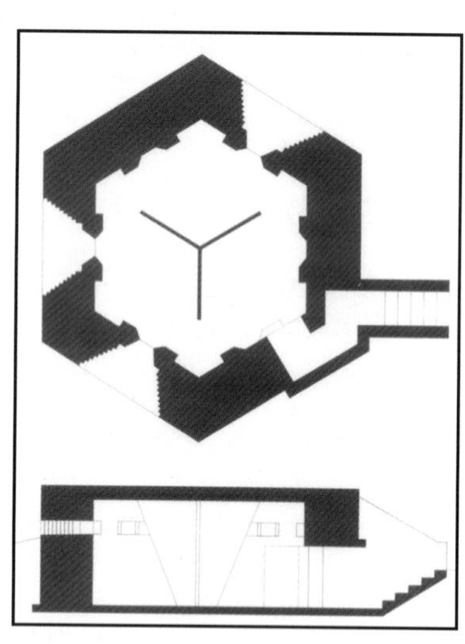

Sywell pillbox

6 AIR DEFENCE IN THE TWO WORLD WARS

World War I saw the beginnings of aerial bombardment, and hence the need to defend against, first enemy airships, and, later on, aircraft. The East Midlands was both attractive as a target with much important war production being carried on, and accessible from the airfields of Belgium and northern Germany. The lessons of this war were carried into the next, and, as the threat was perceived to be greater, much more effort and ingenuity went into countering it. Anti-aircraft guns, which had fortunately, moved on from the improvisations of World War I, were aided by radar, searchlights, spotting, and intelligence. The use of camouflage and other forms of deception such as decoy airfields, were exploited to the full, whilst Air Raid Precautions [ARP], further developed the passive defence element.

ANTI-AIRCRAFT DEFENCE IN WORLD WAR I

Whilst guns designed to shoot down balloons had been developed by 1870, the whole notion of the need for widespread defence against enemy air attack was novel. We have seen how aircraft were deployed against Zeppelins. As the airships were followed by Gotha bombers, the need for dedicated anti-aircraft [AA] guns became more apparent. A whole range of weapons was thrown into action on the basis that nothing of a specialist nature was available. These ranged from machine-guns to 6" howitzers, from naval pom-poms, 3 and 6 pounder guns, to undelivered orders for foreign navies. From field-guns jacked up on precarious towers of logs and cartwheels to coast-defence guns on high-angle mountings. Many guns presented loading difficulties at maximum elevation, and much of the ammunition available was unsuitable, or downright dangerous. Any shell which only burst on contact was a hazard to anything at ground level

WARMINGTON [Northants.]. Control blockhouse for Q Bombing Decoy site, built 1940/1 to protect RAF Kingscliffe; TL080919.

once it had missed its target, and, throughout the War, most shells still did miss their targets.

The strategy behind the distribution of AA defences in World War I, was tied to the expectation that enemy bombing would be directed at specific military targets. Thus, in the East Midlands, AA protection was provided for the Admiralty Wireless Telegraphy [W/T] station at Cleethorpes [Lincs.]; the Royal Naval Air Service airship base at Cranwell [Lincs.]; Derby with its vital munitions plants; the Humber estuary with its W/T station at Waltham; Killingholme's oil-storage tanks and seaplane base, and docks on both sides of the river; Lincoln, Nottingham and Scunthorpe with their munitions factories. The weapons emplaced demonstrate the paucity of what was available. In 1914, a 1 pounder pom-pom defended Cleethorpes W/T station. Killingholme had two of these plus a brace of naval 6 pounder Hotchkiss guns in 1916. A number of 12 pounder coast defence guns were deployed around Lincoln, Nottingham and Derby, in 1917.

METHERINGHAM [Lincs.]. Emergency Railway Control Centre, designed to operate under bombing attack; TFO77614.

Cranwell and Scunthorpe were given the experimental 18 pounder guns with 3″ sleeves, firing 13 pound shells, but enabling the larger cartridge to give maximum propulsion. Only in 1916, was the 3″ 20 cwt. gun available in numbers for home defence. This was seen as the most effective AA gun of the War, and appears in our region on some of the Humber gun-sites, and around Nottingham. A number of the region's AA defences were tested. In October, 1916, two 6 pounder Nordenfeldt guns fired on airships near Corby, as had guns in Nottingham, the previous month.

ANTI-AIRCRAFT DEFENCE IN WORLD WAR II.

By the time that World War II was approaching, the old 3″ 20 cwt. AA gun was still around in numbers, but, in 1934 a new Heavy AA [HAA] weapon - the 3.7″ gun, had been developed by Vickers, and entered service in 1938. Many TA units had been re-organised to man these guns, or the searchlights to go with them. Derby's new Kingsway TA Centre housed the HQ of the 2nd AA Division. In August 1939, the TA AA units were ordered to report to their drill halls across the region. Throughout 1939 and 1940, regimental diaries record how periods of operational duty were interspersed with training activities at the Militia Camps at Ashwell [Rutland], Newark [Notts.], Thrapston [Northants.], and Corringham Rd, Gainsborough [Lincs.].

Early in the War, HAA guns were deployed to protect key industrial targets. Thus Derby and Nottingham, and the Humber Estuary all had HAA cover. Many had LAA as well, as at Spondon [Derbys.] defended by four 40mm Bofors and four Lewis Guns, in October 1940. At Newark [Notts.] a tower for a 40mm Bofors LAA gun survives in the Council Depot in Kelham Road. It consists of a rectangular, single-storey, brick and concrete, reinforced building, where the gun was emplaced on the roof, with ready-use ammunition lockers alongside. As in World War I, some communications centres were protected, but only the old 3" guns were available for the Daventry radio transmitter. Corby started off with only light cover from 34 Lewis Guns, not receiving HAA protection until 1942, when two batteries of 3.7" guns appeared. One or two RAF stations were given HAA guns, North Coates for instance, but the majority made do with LAA guns, sometimes 40mm Bofors, as at Scampton and Waddington, but, more often than not, old World War I Lewis guns on extemporised AA mountings. Binbrook, for example, had 16 Lewis Guns in 1940, but by 1943, these had been replaced by four 40mm Bofors guns, whilst Kirton-in-Lindsey, along with its 15 Lewis Guns, had two old 3" guns in 1940, but never received anything better. In late-1940, the Nottingham and Derby Gun-Defended Area [GDA] had forty 3.7" guns as well as some old 3" guns around the Rolls-Royce plant. This was the same level of provision as enjoyed by Manchester, Portsmouth, and Coventry. One of the Derby sites still survives at Elvaston, where two HAA gun-pits may be seen. By 1942, HAA guns had been emplaced around several more targets - Lincoln, Grantham, Leicester, and Scunthorpe. During the course of the War, 48 different gun-sites were in operation north and south of the Humber,

MABLETHORPE [Lincs.]. ARP Reporting Centre, designed to co-ordinate the response of the emergency services to bombing raids; TF510848.

whilst 12 sites protected Scunthorpe. Along with gun-laying radar, heavier guns appeared, particularly in the Humber GDA, which had 4.5" guns from 1942, and 5.25" from 1944. Examples of HAA sites can still be seen in the region. A 3.7" gun site outside Grantham [H2], for instance, and a 5.25" site near Stalingborough [H20]. It must be remembered, though, that many of the hundred or so HAA sites in our region, will have been equipped only with mobile guns, and remains, therefore, will be minimal. Even less remains of Z Batteries. The 3" Unrotated Rocket Projectile was fired from tubes in multiples of eight, mounted on small, concrete pads. They were manned by the Home Guard. The Women's Auxiliary Air Force was responsible for Barrage Balloons. These were tethered to concrete blocks, or winched off the backs of trucks. No.7 Balloon Centre, one of 18 such depots across the country, was at Alvaston [Derbys.] with its HQ on the corner of Midland Road and Carrington Street, in Derby.

Changing threats demanded frequent re-deployments of the guns. An early example is the response to the Baedeker raids of early 1942, when Lincoln got its HAA defences. In April 1944, Lincoln and Grantham lost their guns to the

SUTTON BASSETT [Northants], Observer Corps WWII aircraft spotting post. Above the door is an open platform, originally reached by an external ladder. Inside are two bunks; the post-War underground post is adjacent; SE789045.

Diver anti-V1 defences in the South of England, and up the East Coast. Later, a bigger shift came in Autumn, 1944, when these defences were extended northwards from Skegness [Lincs.] as the *Diver Fringe*. Twelve HAA sites were staffed by the men and women of 144 Regiment RA, with HQ at South Elkington Hall, and a Sector Operations Room at Louth Park, where a close-defence pillbox still survives. These sites each consisted of four 3.7" guns mounted on Pile mattresses, specially designed for both stability, and speed of construction. The guns stood in line, facing out to sea, and were directed via gun-laying radar. In a monumental effort before the onset of winter, all accommodation was moved from tents into Nissen huts. One of these Diver sites stood on Mablethorpe sea-front. There were Battery HQs at Trusthorpe holiday camp, and at The Camp, Marsh Chapel. Along with the HAA guns, searchlights and LAA were also deployed against the flying bombs.

OUNDLE [Northants.]. Possible Gas Decontamination building, this could be a post-War Civil Defence Centre; TL044883.

As well as AA gun-sites, there were searchlight sites. These began as permanent sites, early on in the War, but quickly shifted to being mobile. Thus there are literally hundreds of some-time searchlight sites in our region. In July 1940, AA Brigade HQs ordered that searchlight sites must be 'wired and dug in for all-round defence'. Further, a pillbox must be built at each site. Consequently, many of these early sites may be located by the presence of an otherwise unexplained pillbox. There are lines of searchlight sites traceable thus, for instance:

- across the area south-east of Nottingham, from Stathern to Gotham, with four pillboxes remaining from six sites [4/6].
- running west, from east of Stamford, from Ketton to Launde [Rutland] [5/5].
- running in a loop on a 5 mile radius of Corby [Northants.] [5/?].
- forming an arc to the north of Melton Mowbray [4/?].

Throughout the War, experimentation was taking place to find the most effective and efficient ways of deploying lights, in relation both to guns and to aircraft put up to intercept bombers. In October 1940, eight sites in north Lincolnshire, in two groups centred on Scunthorpe, were each given six lights and a sound locator.

ANTI-AIRCRAFT RADAR IN WORLD WAR II

Britain entered the War with a network of Radio Direction Finding [RDF] sites, which stretched right down the eastern side of the country. Part of the initial development of this system had taken place in February 1935, in Northamptonshire, when a radio signal, transmitted from the BBC masts on Borough Hill, Daventry, reflected off a Heyford bomber, and was picked up on equipment in a van parked near Weedon. By the outbreak of War, the English Chain Home [CH] stations extended from Northumberland to the Isle of Wight. Each radar station consisted of a transmitter block with four, 350" high, steel towers in line, and a receiver block, inside a square of four, 240" high, timber towers. An example of such a radar station, in our region, was No.34-Stenigot [Lincs.], where one of the steel towers, the

STENIGOT (Lincs.]. The standard Radar site guardroom; TF257825.

two underground blocks, guardroom, site warden's bungalow, and other buildings remain, under some degree of ancient monument protection. More practical, war-time protection was provided by close defence pillboxes, two of which remain. It had become apparent that low-flying enemy aircraft could not be picked up by the CH stations, so supplementary radar installations called CH Low [CHL] were

STENIGOT [Lincs.]. The surviving steel Transmitter mast; TF256826.

built, usually paired with a CH station. No.33-Ingoldmells [Lincs.] opened in February 1940, and No.34A-Skendleby, in June 1941. CHL transmitters and receivers operated in the form of rotating, mesh screens, mounted on gantries built over brick huts. These were generally surrounded by earth traverses to minimise blast damage from bombing. A guard hut, generator, and basic accommodation completed the station. During the invasion scare, it had been intended that the army would proceed independently with its own Coast Defence CHL system to cover particularly vulnerable beaches. Four sites in Lincolnshire were identified - Donna Nook, Mablethorpe, Huttoft Bank, and Chapel St Leonards. It was quickly realised how wasteful this would be, and these sites received temporary, multi-purpose equipment. By the end of 1942, the Mablethorpe radar was deemed redundant. At the same time, Skendleby was equipped with new radar sets and designated CHE[xtra]L. At Humberston [Lincs.] a new Air Ministry Triple Service CHL station was built in 1941, with a 184" high tower, the normal gantry system proving unsuitable for such a low-lying location. Donna Nook was closed by January 1944.

Another major development was aimed at directing fighters onto enemy bombers by radar. This was known as Ground Control Interception [GCI], and was originally based on mobile equipment. The GCI station at Orby [Lincs.] opened in January 1941, to aid fighters from, amongst other bases, RAF Digby. By the end of 1943, Orby was a permanent station, and had been joined by Langtoft [Lincs.]. A mobile station was located at Staythorpe, now Southwell Racecourse [Notts.]. Orby and Langtoft each had a 30" long aerial gantry, mounted over an underground chamber, housing a motor for rotating the aerials, and the transmitter equipment. The operations room, two storeys high at one end, measured roughly 150' by 40'. It was christened the 'Happidrome', and, apart from the aerial array, and generator, contained all the functions of the site under one roof. One survives at Langtoft. One last technological development must be recorded here. Over Spalding, early in the War, an Avro Anson, picked up the navigational aid in the form of a radio-beam, which enabled German bombers to reach their targets. It was code-named Knickebein. British retaliation took the form of a transmitter which inserted extra dashes into the German signal, confusing the navigators. This was code-named Aspirin and the transmitter was at Holton-le-Moor [Lincs.]. A later scheme based in Louth [Lincs.] corrupted the German signals and then replicated them, receiving at Legbourne, and transmitting from South Elkington [Lincs.]. The British equivalent of Knickebein was Gee, transmitted from stations at Nettleton and Stenigot [Lincs.]. A hut, standing until recently, at Stenigot, was a base for Gee operations, as was a brick building standing alongside the A16 road near Ulceby Cross [Lincs.].

THE [ROYAL] OBSERVER CORPS [ROC] IN WORLD WAR II

Experience gained in the London Air Defence Area in World War I, highlighted the effectiveness of aircraft spotters, in warning of enemy air-raids. It was decided that a country-

CLEETHORPES [Lincs.]. The World War I air-raid shelter in Yarra Road, now used as a lock-up garage; approx. TA309085.

wide network of visual spotting-posts, manned by volunteers, should be set up to supplement radar and AA sound-location, in the identification of attacks by enemy bombers. In 1935, ROC Groups were established in the southern half of the country. Northamptonshire's posts, for the most part, came under No. 12 Group in Bedford, with a few under No. 15 Group in Cambridge. On 1st March 1936, No. 11 Group was formed by the Chief Constable in Lincoln with HQ at the Telephone Exchange. The provision in our region was completed in 1938, with the formation of No.6 Group in Derby. One or two outliers came under Coventry [No.5 Group], Manchester [No.7 Group], or York [No.8 Group]. Common equipment in each post was used to plot the height, location and course of aircraft. Information was sent via the local HQ to a Fighter Command Operations Room, from which, in the case of Lincoln, for instance, the fighters at RAF Digby would be scrambled. No. 12 Fighter Group had its operations centre at Watnall [Notts.], where a Filter Room assembled all the available data from all sources, and attempted to identify priorities. This building at Watnall still stands, deep in a wooded hollow with protection from a close-defence pillbox, and a loop-holed blockhouse, once part of the demolished guardroom.

The posts themselves took a variety of forms. The basic design was a wooden hut, a bit bigger than the average garden-shed. This housed a telephone connection, and basic domestic requirements- kettle, bedding, Elsan etc. A timber platform nearby held a map table and the plotting instrument, to which was later added the Micklethwaite height-correction attachment. The basic plotting instrument stayed in use for nearly 25 years. One or two refinements occasionally appeared, such as microphone gas-masks, but the whole operation was generally very low-tech. If more suitable locations presented themselves as the spotting platform, then they were used. Church towers and windmills were popular. The top of the water-tower of Sleaford Maltings [Lincs.], reached by 240 steps, certainly gave added height. In Northamptonshire, windmills were in use as informal Home Guard/ROC posts at Barby, Silverstone and Wootton. The roof of the fire station at Upper Mounts, Northampton, was also used as it was the tallest building around. As the War took its course, it was found that the flimsy structures provided earlier, were not up to the job. Although the timber sleeping huts were often retained, the open timber or even sand-bagged platforms were often replaced by quite substantial structures. Photo's taken at the time show brick, two-storey, non-standard blockhouses with upper platforms at Billingborough, Bourne and Mablethorpe [Lincs.]. Such structures survive at Clipston and at Sutton Bassett [Northants.] Several posts in Lincolnshire, Winterton and Louth, for instance, have a standard Home Guard brick store on site, and it would appear that these were built to replace the sleeping hut. As well as changes to the posts, the HQs also changed. In Lincoln, the telephone exchange attic proved cramped so a move was made, first to St Peter's Chambers, Silver Street, in 1940, then, three years later, to St Martin's Hall, Beaumont Fee. It should be noted here that there were also frequent changes in personnel, as youngsters were called up for the forces. New entrants were often expert in the identification of aircraft. In 1942, Oundle School's Spotters' Club had 125 members. In 1941, King George VI granted the 'Royal' prefix. The ROC continued in its role up to the end of the Cold War.

BOMBING DECOYS

Even if it were often impossible to prevent the bombers getting through, at least, an attempt could be made to persuade them to drop their bombs in the wrong place. To this end, a variety of decoy types were constructed. The first perceived targets of enemy attack were the airfields of the RAF. Two sorts of decoy were developed, one, the 'K' was a dummy airfield, complete with dummy aircraft built by the film industry. Here, a team of 20 airmen attempted to convey a working airfield - moving the dummies around, making visible tracks etc. This was to deceive the enemy in daylight. The 'Q' site simulated landing lights at night. [There were also 'QF'- night fires, and 'QL'- night-lights]. Here, the two crew listened for the engines of incoming enemy bombers, and then, once they thought they could be seen, quickly extinguished their lights, as if in alarm. The crew were provided with a brick and concrete blockhouse, from which to control the lights, and for shelter. On top was often a chance light which simulated aircraft taxiing. This blockhouse was often the only substantial structure on the site, and, consequently, all, if anything, that remains. Such blockhouses can be seen at Warmington [Northants], which was a 'Q' site for RAF Kingscliffe. Another, similar blockhouse can be seen at Gautby [Lincs.] a 'K' site for RAF Waddington, which was equipped with dummy Fairey Battle aircraft. Apparently, the set-up, deemed unconvincing, was closed down by August 1942, after only a year in operation. Similar, again, is the blockhouse, recently identified at Braceby [Lincs.] which served RAF Spitalgate. Life on a decoy site-uncomfortable, tedious, and, very often, extremely dangerous, has been described by Geoff Hall and Doug Feary, who served at Hagnaby [Lincs.] a 'K' site for RAF Manby. Of the 231 airfields which had decoys, 20 were in Lincolnshire, and another half-dozen in the rest of our region.

It soon became apparent that there were targets, other than airfields, which could benefit from the provision of decoys. As the raids on urban areas developed, so the 'Starfish' decoy appeared. This was a whole complex of basket fires, large braziers which could be ignited electrically to simulate incendiaries dropping on buildings, and lure bombers away from their real target cities. A whole range of sophisticated fires was developed to simulate every possible bombing scenario. In our region, there were permanent 'Starfish' sites at:

No.4 Derby [Ticknall, Diseworth & Swarkstone; later 'C' Series at Thulston].
No.24 Scunthorpe [Risby, Twigmoor & Brumby].
No.28 Leicester [Galby, Beeby, Newton Harcourt & Willoughby Waterless]
No.30 Nottingham [Clipston, Barton in Fabis, Cropwell Butler & Lowdham]
No.45 Northampton [Kislingbury & Hardingstone].

there were temporary 'Starfish' sites at:

No.52 Lincoln [Branston Fen & Canwick].
No.80 Grantham [Boothby Pagnell].

Most of these were in operation by early 1941, but were redundant by mid 1942, some to be developed into later types, and to operate thus through 1943. In late 1942 decoys had become much more sophisticated, and a list of 'Strategic QL' sites was issued, to show that specific decoy sites were providing specialist decoy lighting for a whole range of industrial sites. Some examples from our region are:

Ambaston, marshalling yard/factory lights, Rolls-Royce Derby
Swarkstone, factory lights/loco glows, Qualcast Ltd, Derby
Lowdham, marshalling yard/loco glows, Gedling Colliery, Nottingham
Risby, factory lights/loco glows, Northern Iron & Steel, Scunthorpe
Cranford, marshalling yard/factory lights, railway station, Kettering
Woodford, factory lights/loco glows, Islip factory, Kettering
Stanion, factory lights/loco glows, Stewart & Lloyd, Corby
Beeby, loco glows/factory lights, London Rd marshalling yards, Leicester
Knotting, marshalling yards/loco glows, marshalling yard, Wellingborough

Army decoys ['A' Series] were provided for certain key depots or ordnance plants:

17 Diseworth	QF/QL	Toton depot [Leics.]
26 Preston Capes	QF	Weedon depot [Northants.]
35 Boothby Pagnell [Lincs.]	QF/QL	Grantham munitions factories
41 Barton in Farbis [Notts.]	Starfish	Chilwellordnancedepot

Some naval installations were provided with decoys. There were a number of decoy sites- 'Starfish', 'QL' & 'QF', on the south bank of the Humber, around Immingham, Grimsby and Humberston. At East Halton [Lincs.] there was a naval 'QF' decoy ['N' Series] and, close by, a 'P' Series oil decoy for the Killingholme fuel depot. These oil decoys, intended to simulate burning tank-farms, were as difficult as any which had been attempted. One problem was that of avoiding burning too much oil and thereby saving the enemy the trouble of bombing the real tanks.

As in any preventative measure it is impossible accurately to quantify success. In May 1941, a raid on Derby was foiled by jamming the German bombers' direction-finding beam; this was fortunate as the decoys would not have worked in time. A raid intended for Nottingham, in the same month, ended up dropping 500 bombs on the village of Plungar and the countryside of the Vale of Belvoir, apparently inexplicably. It was privately speculated, at the time, that the bombers had mistaken the Cropwell Butler 'Starfish'for a burning Nottingham. In their mental map, Plungar thus became the area of Derby containing the Rolls-Royce works. What is known, is that some 300 odd decoy sites out of the 800 or so built, actually drew enemy bombs. It seems you can fool some of the pilots some of the time. There is, of course, the story, often told and possibly apocryphal, of the decoy site receiving a hit from a wooden bomb.

AIR RAID PRECAUTIONS [ARP]

In 1916, a number of raids by Zeppelins on towns around the Humber caused casualties amongst military and civilian alike. It may have been fear of a repetition that caused a pharmacist on Yarra Road, Cleethorpes [Lincs.] to build himself an air-raid shelter. It still stands, now converted to a lock-up garage. Protection against air-raids had not been provided in World War 1, but such was the fear of bombing, that thinking about civilians at risk had begun as early as 1924. However, ARP as an institution, did not get up and running until 1935, and not until the summer of 1939, was there any published guidance on the construction of shel-

RUSHDEN [Northants.]. Fire-watcher's post; now standing in the old railway station yard, next to the Home Guard office; SP956672.

ters. The only public provision was to be for those caught in the open in a raid. All other shelters were to be provided at home, or at work. Boots in Nottingham was one of the few employers who responded to the Government's message by providing shelters for their work-force, early in the War. It was to become, under the terms of the 1939 Defence Act, compulsory for all employers of more than 50 workers, to provide shelters for them. Nottingham's public shelters could accommodate 36000 people and were almost exclusively in the city centre. Derby's held 7000. The bulk of shelters were to be domestic, and it is these- Anderson shelters, for instance, which are best remembered. Given that some 2.5 million of these were issued, only a remarkably small number remains. Many shelters were merely basements with some degree of strengthening and an emergency exit. Surface shelters were built to serve certain streets or blocks of flats. Many of these were substandard, and heavy rain was known to wash out the mortar, leading to collapse. Contemporary photo's show communal surface shelters being built in Derby, Nottingham, Lincoln, Leicester and Grantham. Brick huts with concrete roofs were provided as Wardens' posts, and this design was also used for Home Guard explosives and inflammables stores. At Newark, there is an underground hospital underneath the RHP Bearings factory in Northern Road. Forgotten since the War, it was rediscovered in June 2000. The factory was bombed in 1941, so the hospital may have been used then, or built as a response to future raids. It is entered through a decontamination centre, so it would appear to have been built early in the War, when the danger of a gas attack was particularly feared. Each town or locality had an ARP Reporting Centre which collated reports of injuries and damage, and organised the response by the emergency services. That in Mablethorpe still survives, in brick with concrete roof, and water-tower, next door to the town's fire station. Another interesting survival is the Railway Control Centre, beside the level-crossing in Metheringham [Lincs.]. This is a single-storey building in brick, with a thick, concrete roof, and small windows which, originally, probably had steel shutters. This Centre controlled the movements of all rail traffic over a wide area in the event of an emergency. Small, one-man, steel shelters for ARP Wardens, sentries, or police officers were made by Rustons of Lincoln. One stands in a field in Skellingthorpe [Lincs.], there was one reported in Spondon [Derbys.], and similar examples can be seen at Duxford Imperial War Museum, and at RAF Manston in Kent where it is attributed to the ROC. Observation is not the activity one would most obviously associate with it. Another version, identified as a "Consol" shelter, but more like a deactivated Dalek, stands outside the old railway station in Rushden [Northants.], beside the re- created Home Guard HQ. Air-raid shelters are often found, tucked away in people's back-gardens, and, that, coupled with the fact that there was no official record of the number of shelters built- only the number of people provided for, means that it is difficult to gauge survival rates. If only 5% survive though, given the vast numbers involved, an awful lot must still be out there.

Paul Mould grew up in Boston [Lincs.] during World War II, and lists, in his account of the experience, the ARP provision for the town.

- 7 air-raid warning SIRENS.
- 46 public air-raid SHELTERS, some in cellars, some on the surface.
- A central FIRE-STATION and 2 sub-stations.
- A HOSPITAL [1A] and Isolation Hospital, plus 2 ARP FIRST-AID posts.
- 2 emergency temporary shelters for the HOMELESS.

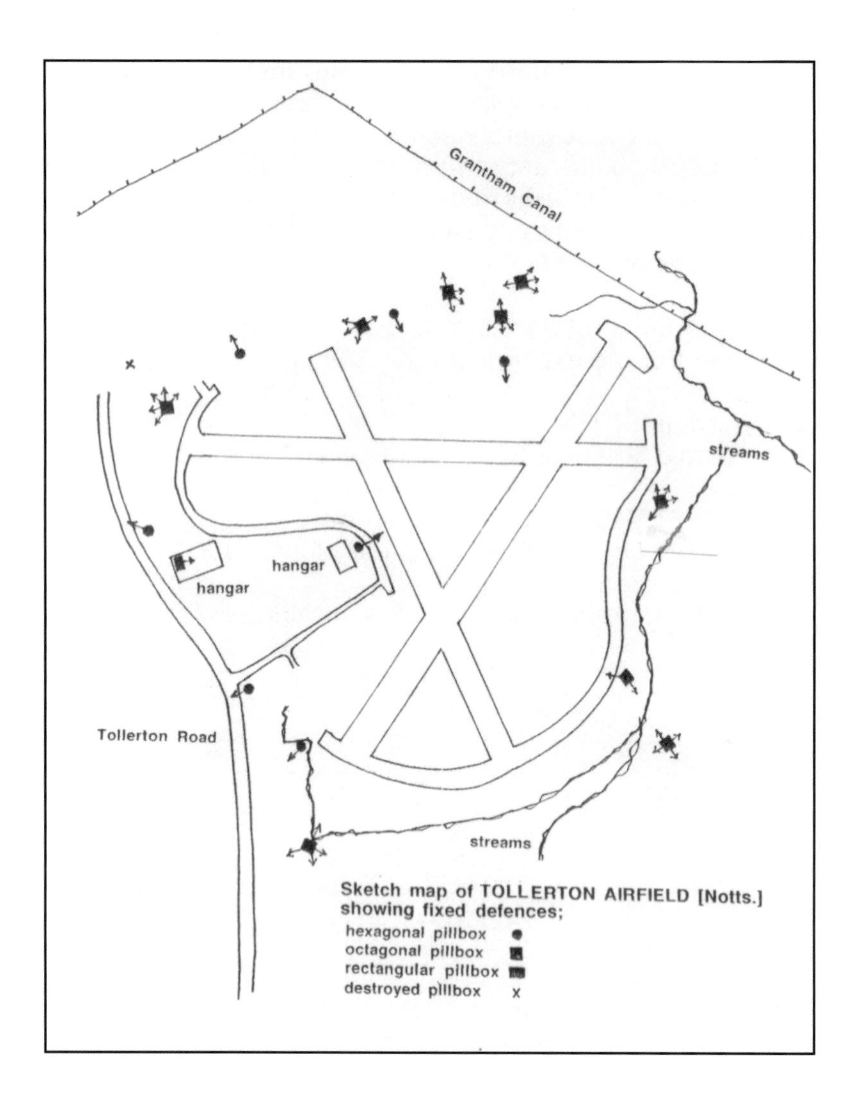

Sketch map of TOLLERTON AIRFIELD [Notts.] showing fixed defences;

STENIGOT CHAIN-HOME RADAR STATION, LINCOLNSHIRE

Stenigot was built as part of the original air-defence RDF [radar] system of 20 such stations extending from the Isle of Wight, up the east coast to the north of Scotland. Started in summer 1938, Stenigot, within the year, consisted of a line of four 240' [74m] timber receiver towers, and a square of four 350' [108m] steel transmitter towers. Transmitter and receiver blocks were semi-sunken, and an older set of equipment - the buried reserve, was installed underground for emergency use. A guardroom, caretaker's house, generator completed the site, all within a defended perimeter. The towers were self-supporting, with their feet standing on concrete blocks on deep foundations. Right up to the outbreak of war, and throughout the war, there was a programme of constant review, adaptation of equipment, and improvement in operation. As allied planes were equipped with transponders, for instance, then RDF stations could tell friend from foe. Later developments such as Gee were also set up at Stenigot.

Stenigot RDF Station: the Transmitter Block

During the Cold War, an array of radar dishes was set up as part of Ace High, the NATO communications system carrying air-defence data between NATO sites. The site now consists of one transmitter tower, transmitter and receiver blocks, guard-room, house and two pillboxes. The dishes have been toppled, and all the other buildings demolished.

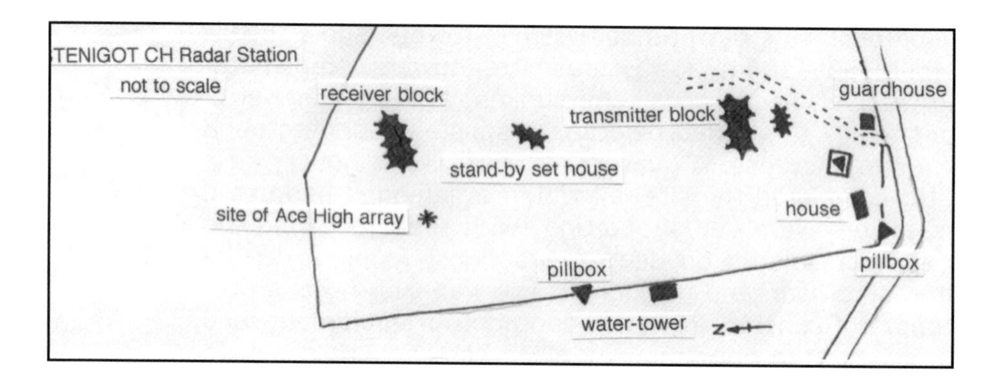

7

THE COLD WAR

In 1945, a bankrupt Britain, with a country to rebuild, a work-force to retrain, and an economy to revitalise, could spare little for maintaining a conventional defence capability, let alone developing one based on nuclear weapons. However, the days of the conventional battlefield were seen to be over, and, like it or not, some credible and realistic defence policy for the nuclear age was expected. In the event, the decision was taken to focus on the strategic nuclear deterrent, and this was seen as an unique role for the RAF, and it was this element which received the bulk of defence funding until 1969. By the mid-1950s, a nuclear attack from the USSR was feasible, but, despite the development of the expensive ROTOR system, an effective anti-aircraft capability was not seen as attainable, and AA Command was stood down in 1958. Coast Artillery had gone earlier, in 1956. The early-1950s had seen the introduction of effective surface-to-air missiles [SAMs], and these, along with the jet-fighters, were seen as a defence for the bomber bases. By 1961, a Defence Review concluded that Britain was still overspending. One solution was seen as the long-range delivery of nuclear warheads via missiles - the THOR system. This lasted only into the early-1960s. Eventually the missile option was to be effected through the nuclear submarines of the Royal Navy. In the meantime, the nuclear deterrent stayed with the RAF and its V-Bombers, many of which were based in our region, along with the secure bomb storage. Alongside a nuclear response capability was needed an early-warning system, and here the Royal Observer Corps [ROC], in a new incarnation, were teamed with the United Kingdom Warning and Monitoring Organisation [UKWMO]. Time, in all this, was of the essence, and a national system of communications enabled news to travel fast via the Post Office Towers. The final piece in this jigsaw was a network of emergency centres of national, regional and local government, to come into operation only after a nuclear strike. Most of the above elements were represented in the field in our region, and this chapter is concerned with what there was, and with how much of it remains.

THE RAF IN THE NUCLEAR-AGE

In a direct continuation of the role of the World War II bomber bases, much of the RAF's nuclear capability was based in Lincolnshire. The key bases were Scampton, Waddington, Coningsby [Lincs.], flying Vulcans, and Cottesmore [Leics.], with Victors. These operated from the late 1950s, as part of a Quick Reaction Alert [QRA] force, maintaining a proportion of each squadron on 15 minutes stand-by, some aircraft being parked on concrete Operational Readiness Platforms. Equipped with Blue Steel stand-off bombs, the V-bombers could launch 100 miles from their ultimate

ELVASTON [Derbys.]. Anti-Aircraft Operations Room, built early 1950s to control the AA defences of Nottingham & Derby; it is on the site of a World War II HAA Battery, of which two emplacements survive on a campsite; SK403326.

target. This situation continued until 1969, when the Navy took over with Polaris. Developments on the ground to support the new aerial technology can be seen at all those RAF stations. Longer runways were necessary, and at both Waddington, and, more spectacularly, at Scampton, the old Roman road, the A15, had to be diverted in order to accommodate the runway extensions. Coningsby was closed for three years from November 1964, to be expanded for the anticipated arrival of the TSR2. Instead, the Phantoms arrived. Waddington received a new operations block, and new electronics workshops in the 1950s, At Waddington, the old Watch Office was adapted for approach control, and a new one, to drawing number 7378a/55 was built for local control. At Swinderby, the full 7378a/55 design was built for side-by-side local and approach control - the only one in the UK. Many airfields were brought up-to-date, either by adding a new Visual Control Room [VCR] to drawing number 5871 c/55, to the existing tower, as at Barkston Heath, Coningsby, Cranwell, Scampton and Strubby [Lincs.], and Cottesmore and North Luffenham [Leics.], or by building from scratch at Manby [2548c/55], and, as we have seen at Waddington and Swinderby [Lincs.]. At Langar [Notts.], a non-standard VCR was added to the tower. All these towers still stand. The nuclear bomb-Blue Steel, needed specialist buildings for the weapons system and its fuel. These can be seen at Scampton and Waddington. At Coningsby, a Gaydon hangar, to hold V-bombers can be seen, and, in 1981 the first hardened aircraft shelters in the region were built here. The fighters, deployed to protect the V-bombers, were based at Binbrook [Lincs.], at one time Javelins and later, Lightnings. Here, there is a 1972 QRA hangar, designed for a pair of armed Lightnings to be on 24-hour stand-by. A similar hangar awaits re-assembly at the air museum at Bruntingthorpe [Leics.], where there is also a post-World War 11 USAF hangar, dating from the airfield's occupation from 1953 to 1962. The runway here was lengthened to 3400 yards [3140 metres], to take the B-47 bomber. At Cranwell [Lincs.] stands a RUB demountable hangar, harking back to the World War I Bessoneau.

Although Scampton and Waddington have their own bomb-

FISKERTON [Lincs.]. Pagoda-style Royal Observer Corps Midlands HQ, built 1950s to co-ordinate air defence in the East Midlands; TF046725.

stores, designed for the nuclear bombs of the V-bomber force, and heavily protected by wire fences and watch-towers, the main designated Permanent Ammunition Depot [PAD], was sited, from 1950, on the old airfield at Faidingworth [Lincs.], and was to serve the bases in Lincolnshire - Binbrook, Coningsby, Hemswell, Scampton and Waddington. There are workshops and stores, surrounded by massive clay traverses, all connected with servicing and assembling Blue Steel and its predecessors. In one section are 60 individual brick-built stores the size of garden sheds, which housed Gauntlet, the bomb's initiator, and its batteries. Three large bomb-stores, with gantries in front, each stored 40 nuclear bombs. Via these gantries, bombs were loaded into ordinary RAF trucks for the regular deliveries to the airfields. Around the whole site are triple fences, and one of the twelve watch-towers built for security. The kennels housed semi-wild German Shepherds, some of which roamed between the fences at night. Since its closure in 1972, the site has been used by BMARC of Grantham to test its Oerlikon guns. The target at the end of the long indoor range is mounted on a large chunk of armour-plate from the

World War II battleship Tirpitz, sunk in a Norwegian fjord by bombers from Bardney and Woodhall Spa [Lincs.] in March 1944. At the time of writing, BMARC is re-locating its operations, so maybe the site will become an industrial estate like Barnham, its twin in Norfolk.

As protectors of the V-bombers against air attack, the fighters were complemented by the new SAM squadrons equipped with Bloodhounds. The first operational base was North Coates, where trials continued throughout most of 1958 and well into 1959. Eventually three fire units totalling 48 launchers were mounted. The other SAM sites in our region were Dunholme Lodge and Woodhall Spa [Lincs]. and North Luffenham and Woolfox Lodge [Rutland]. North Luffenham and North Coates were equipped with Yellow River radar for directing the missiles. On the ground, a number of features were visible. The eight launchers in each fire unit were regularly spaced in a 2x4 grid. At some remove were the Launch Control Post, the Works Services Building where the missiles were assembled and maintained, and the other structures necessary for arming and fuelling. This layout is visible at all the stations used, generally superimposed on the runway or perimeter track. All but North Coates, had two fire units. At Dunholme Lodge, the Works Services Building is easily visible, resembling a double barn. Most of the dedicated SAM installations had been shut down by 1965. North Coates continued into the 'seventies, then had a spell in care and maintenance, before being re-activated, in 1976, with Bloodhound IIs from Cyprus and Singapore. Later on, Bloodhounds were redeployed to additional airfields, Barkston Heath, for instance, receiving a flight, returned from Germany in 1983, to defend Cottesmore, by then a Tornado base.

ROTOR- AN AIR-DEFENCE RADAR SYSTEM

In 1948, an attempt was made to rationalise the Radar defences of Britain. It was decided to maintain at least East Coast cover, in order to co-ordinate a response to the encroachment into our airspace by hostile aircraft. This response involved both fighter interceptors and AA artil-

HARBY [Leics.]. Underground Royal Observer Corps monitoring post, one of a network of 1500 such posts built in the early 1960s to plot the fall of atomic bombs, and to measure radio-active fall-out; SK745305.

lery. A network of Chain Home, Chain Home Low, and Chain Home Extra-Low radar stations, in protected structures, was proposed, and partly carried out, during the early 1950s. A number of these installations are in our region. Stenigot [Lincs.] was a Chain Home ROTOR 1 site dating from before World War II. The remaining mast, guardhouse, receiver and transmitter blocks, along with other buildings from this period remain. The recently demolished array of radar dishes were from the later, 1960s, ACE HIGH system. Skendleby [Lincs.] was a Ground Control Interceptor [E] [GCI] ROTOR 1 site. It is in an R3 building with two floors underground, reached by underground passage from the standard, bungalow guardroom. It has subsequently been adapted, and, more recently, sold. The above ground features, however, are quite recognisable. Langtoft [Lincs.] was a GCI [A] ROTOR 1 site. It has an R6 building, which is on two floors, but only partly submerged. Although the guardhouse is standard, there can obviously be no subterranean passage. Also on the site is the 1943 Happidrome, or operations block, from the earlier GCI radar station. Around the site are some of the cubical, concrete plinths which held the radar heads. Three out of the original five plinths for Type

SWALLOW [Lincs.]. The elevated version of the ORLIT aircraft-spotting post introduced in 1952 for use by volunteer observers of the Royal Observer Corps; by 1957 it was felt that aircraft were too fast for visual spotters to register, but some posts in the eastern counties were manned until 1965. This is the only known elevated ORLIT in the region; TA177024.

13 Mark 6 height-finding radars survive. A standard Type 80 radar modulator building stands east of the Happidrome. The site is used as a scrap-yard and is not easily viewed. About two miles north-west is the wireless station, a single-

storey brick building with steel-shuttered windows, in agricultural use. A large estate of married quarters also stands, now private houses. At Watnall [Notts.], the filter block of Fighter Command's 12 Group Sector Operations Centre, built in 1943 as the final component of an installation begun in 1938, stands in a deep cutting. Now surrounded by a natural area of Special Scientific Interest, and encroached on by industrial properties, the forlorn, concrete structure has been used as a gun-club. It continued in use under the ROTOR plan, being up-graded in 1950, until 1961, the date when other sites in our region ceased to be part of ROTOR and its successors. The AA defences were controlled from purpose-built AA Operations Rooms [AAOR] constructed on two levels with two-foot-thick concrete walls and roof. The upper level held offices and canteen, while, below ground was the operations area in a well with surrounding balcony. These structures were only in use for a short while in the mid 1950s. The AAOR for the control of the Nottingham and Derby Gun-Defended Area [GDA], survives at Elvaston [Derbys.], with the remains of an earlier AA battery nearby. The almost featureless, low, concrete building with its porch and ventilation tower, now sits in the middle of a caravan-park. In order to utilise the guidance they were receiving from GCI stations, it was vital that fighter aircraft were able to locate themselves precisely. For this purpose, a network of 79 navigational receivers/transmitters called VHF Fixer Stations was established. Three were in our region, at Beckingham [Notts.], Lutton and Skidbrooke [Lincs.]. At Beckingham, the concrete hut-base survives in the corner of a field.

THE THOR INTERMEDIATE RANGE BALLISTIC MISSILE [IRBM] SYSTEM

THOR was a US missile which could deliver a one megaton nuclear war-head, up to a range of 1500 miles. Based in Europe, it could hit targets which were out of the range of USA-based missiles. The British Blue Streak IRBM would not be ready until the early 1960s at the soonest, and would require underground silos and other costly and time-consuming works. THOR was available in 1958 for deployment

MELTON MOWBRAY [Leics.]. The blast-walls of one of the three THOR pads at this IRBM base; SK749157

on British bases, and little was needed in the way of infrastructure. Old airfields were quite adequate, providing hard-standing. The missile was housed horizontally on a trailer, inside a steel-framed, covered shelter, being raised to the vertical for firing, on its own, in-built, erector cradle. The launch-pads consisted of concrete hard-standings with thick, L-shaped concrete blast-walls. Wiring for the prelaunch functions was led, by underground ducting, from the mobile Launch Control Trailer to each of the site's three pads. A timber guardroom, and a Classified Storage Building inside earth traverses, stood some distance away from the pads. The storage tanks, for the extremely volatile liquid oxygen used to fuel the rocket, stood adjacent to the pad, but the equipment used to pump it under pressure, was brought up on trailers. A small, brick building to house the equipment which set the missile's guidance system was about 125 yards [120 metres] from the rocket. Thus, there was very little to see. Perhaps it was in order to draw attention to this deterrent weapon, that a double-fenced, wire compound was erected round the site, and flood-lit at night. Pilots coming in to land at East Anglian airfields during the

MELTON MOWBRAY [Leics.]. The Gyroscope-setting building of the THOR base; SK749155.

early 1960s, have described how, on clear nights, much of the chain of illuminated THOR sites was visible from the sky. In all, twenty of these sites were built and armed, remaining in service from 1958 until 1963. They were in four clusters, with one site in each cluster having additional facilities for servicing and maintenance. One cluster was in Lincolnshire where Hemswell was the main base for Bardney, Caistor, Coleby Grange, and Ludford Magna. North Luffenham was the main base for Harrington and Polebrook [Northants], Folkingham [Lincs.] and Melton Mowbray [Leics.]. The other clusters were centred on Norfolk and East Yorkshire. North Luffenham is probably the most complete of all the THOR sites, but the prominent blast-walls can still be seen at most of our sites. At Harrington, the Classified Storage Building still sits inside its earth traverses, and the guidance building still stands at Melton Mowbray.

THE ROC AND THE UKWMO IN THE COLD WAR PERIOD

As we have already seen, the ROC had its origins in the mid 1930s as a means of spotting, identifying and reporting

LANGTOFT [Lincs.]. The Bungalow Guardroom standard at ROTOR Ground Control Interceptor radar sites of the early 1950s; TF154130.

hostile aircraft in British airspace. When ROTOR prompted a review of air defence procedures generally, the ROC function was noted. In 1952 the Orlit company produced a design for a new spotting post and over 200 ground-level versions, Type A, and another 200 or so of the elevated, Type B, were erected, some on the ROC's established sites, and some on re-sited or completely new ones. By 1954, when a nuclear attack on Britain by a foreign power was possible, the need was seen for a system for monitoring nuclear fallout. This responsibility was devolved onto the ROC, and after 1965, when it was no longer possible to identify fast-flying aircraft visually, it became their sole function. In 1955, an underground bunker had been designed for the ROC to fulfil this role. Building of these underground posts began in 1958, and by 1965, some 985 had been completed, and all the above-ground posts, closed. The network of posts reported to protected, underground headquarters, each one, initially,

LANGTOFT [Lincs.]. Plinth for Type 13 Mark 6 height-finding radar, One of three remaining in the field near the main building; TF155127.

controlling around 50 posts. The UKWMO was the umbrella organisation, responsible for collating and distributing information, which could both inform the military, and warn the civilian population of impending, or, more likely, imminent nuclear attack. The system, with periodic restructuring lasted until 1991, although many posts had been closed by 1968.

At the end of World War II, there were 1,500 or so ROC posts of varying design. The new Orlit pattern was a rectangular, concrete box, measuring 10' by 7' [3m x 2m]. The covered half was a shelter/store, the open part contained a table and plotting equipment. Type A was designed to sit on foundations at ground-level, Type B was mounted on concrete legs and accessed by an integral ladder. Examples of Type A can be seen at Burgh-on-Bain, and Sturton-by-Stow [Lincs.]. The only Type B built in Lincolnshire was at Swallow.

The underground post which came into service in the late 1950s was a concrete, sealed, box, 19′ by 7′6″ [5.8m x 2.6 m] and with an interior height of 7′6″ [2.3m] buried under three feet of earth. Inside, were two bunks, a chemical toilet, some storage for a week's supply of food and water, and a working space 7′ [2m] square. Its crew of four, two on. two off, would enter through a manhole-type hatch. On the surface, all that is visible is the top of the hatch, basic instrumentation, and air vents. The Fixed Survey Meter would measure radiation levels, the Bomb Power Indicator recorded blast; and the Ground Zero Indicator charted the position of the blast. Communication was by telephone, with one post in each cluster of three being equipped with radio. The superstructure of many of these underground posts can be seen still. There are easily-seen examples at Buckminster [Leics.], Burton Joyce [Notts.], and Winterton [Lincs.]. At Farnsfield [Notts.], the post has been demolished, but a commemorative plaque has been placed in the hedgerow. For those seeking out ROC posts, it must be remembered that many were relocated at different times in their

FALDINGWORTH [Lincs.]. One of the atomic bomb stores at this Permanent Ammunition Depot; approx. TFO26850.

operational lives. Sometimes a good visual spotting site, for instance, did not subsequently lend itself successfully to a subterranean existence. Consequently, a single post may have up to three recorded map references.

The headquarters buildings were re-located underground from around 1962. This meant that Derby's former 6 Group HQ, at first in the GPO Telephone Exchange, and from 1942, at Highfields, The Broadway, was closed. The 15 Group HQ moved from RAF Waddington, where it had been since 1947, to a new, semi-underground, protected structure on the RAF Fiskerton site. This is a 'pagoda' style, entered at ground-level, but with a lower floor containing communications centre, and the well of the operations room, overlooked by a balcony. There is also a range of pre- fabricated SECO hutting, housing the offices for 15 Group, and the whole Midland Region. When the ROC stood down and these buildings became available, they were snapped up by a cartridge-filling firm. It would appear that Northamptonshire posts which survived beyond 1968, were assigned to 7 Group, with HQ at Bedford. Many of the surviving posts in Derbyshire, Leicestershire and Nottinghamshire, belonged to 8 Group, Coventry/Rugby with a protected bunker at Lawford Heath, near the former RAF airfield.

EMERGENCY CONTROL CENTRES AND COMMUNICATIONS

In the event of nuclear war, and in the absence of any civilian shelter provision, it was intended that order would be maintained through the continuation at all levels of government. For this purpose, legislation designated a network of Regional Seats of Government [RSG], which would enact the wishes of central government. In 1952, local authorities were required to set up their own, nuclear fallout-resistant bunkers. The RSG for Region 3, the North Midlands, is within the government office complex at Chalfont Drive, in Nottingham. The 1950s War Room, on two floors, with very limited accommodation for only key personnel and full-height map-room, was encased in five-foot-thick [1.5m] concrete walls, with a roof, seven-foot thick [2.2m]. As planning pro-

WOOLFOX LODGE [Rutland]. The assembly shed for the RAM jets of the Bloodhound surface-to-air missiles based here in the 1960s; SK960127.

gressed, and it was realised that any post-Bomb operation would continue for months rather than days, further facilities were added, more domestic accommodation for more personnel, and specialist features like BBC studios, from which to communicate to any survivors out there. At Nottingham, in the 1960s, an extra floor was added, on stilts over the existing earlier structure, to meet the increased requirements of the 1958 RSG programme. In 1966, a re-assessment of likely targets and their relative vulnerabilities, resulted in a further clutch of bunkers, labelled Sub-Regional Controls [S-RC]. The former ROTOR radar blockhouse at Skendleby, for Sub-Region 31, and, for Sub-Region 32, an ex-World War II Cold Store in Loughborough, were selected for this function. The Skendleby site continued for a long time in this role, even receiving a major re-fit in 1985, under the Thatcher government's enthusiastic embrace of the Cold War. The local authorities responded to the requirement on them to provide bomb-proof council offices in a variety of ways. Some started early, while others only acted as lately as 1987, when the Home Office offered

WOOLFOX LODGE [Rutland]. The Arming shed for the surface-to-air Bloodhound missiles based here in the 1960s; SK955134.

100% funding. Leicestershire incorporated a radiation-proof basement in 1968, in its new Glenfield complex. Charnwood District Council built a standard, post-1982 nuclear bunker under their office extension in Loughborough, around 1990. Melton Mowbray's bunker, was built under the new offices in the late-1980s. Nottinghamshire had a small emergency centre under the 1960's County Hall extension in West Bridgford, also sharing Severn-Trent Water's emergency control centre under their head office in Mansfield. Mansfield District Council has an emergency centre under its 1990 Civic Centre. Rutland has no provision other than at Glenfield, where emergency planning is shared with Leicestershire. In Lincolnshire, there are emergency centres in council office basements in Lincoln, Brigg, and Grantham. County Hall in Northampton, housed the County's emergency centre, until replaced, in the 1980s by a new Centre under the County Record Office at Wootton Hall. Northampton County Hall then became the Stand-by Centre, itself replacing the Social Services Offices in Kettering. Elsewhere in the county, Wellingborough's new combined Fire and Ambulance Station, in 1962, included a Civil Defence HQ below. Derbyshire has its emergency centre under the offices in Matlock. Most of these bunkers are simply large suites of rooms buried under a few feet of concrete, provided with ventilation and restricted access. They contain communications equipment, and supplies for, in the case of a County, up to 80 staff, including military HQ personnel, and police liaison officers, to work. In recognition of the disruption to food distribution that a nuclear attack would cause, emergency food Supply and Transport Stores were set up by the Home Office. In Region 3, these were at Desborough Airfield and Weedon Depot [Northants.], Burton Road, Branston, and North Willingham [Lincs.]. The Ministry of Agriculture, Fisheries and Food [MAFF] maintained a network of Buffer Depots, but could not have held more than a couple of weeks' supplies.

The following, were in Region 3:

336	Main Road, Smalley Gate, Notts.
336HJ	New Street, Earl Shilton, Leics.
336K	Little Glen Road, Glen Parva, Leics.
336M	Humberstone Lane, Thurmaston, Leics.
336N	Hariestone Road, New Dunston, Northants.
336T	Coxmoor Road, Sutton-in-Ashfield, Notts.
559A	Crick Road, Hilmorton, Northants.
-	Memory Lane, Belgrave Gate, Leicester.
-	Mackin Street, Derby.
-	Fiskerton Airfield, Lincoln.
-	Station Road, Castle Donington, Leics.
336P	New Unit 70, 10 Romany Way, Market Har borough, Leics.

MAFF consistently declined to make public the full extent of its emergency planning either by location, or by capacity,so the above is not a complete list. At Immingham was an underground oil storage depot. By the early-1980s, an extensive telecommunications system, linking all the S-RCS,had been completed. This had been planned, back in 1954, and included the BT microwave tower network, whose best known example is in London's Tottenham Court Road. Such towers stand at Kirkby Underwood, Carlto Scroop, and Claxby [Lincs.]. A spur of the microwave link, often referred to as BACKBONE, runs through Oakham, Copt Oak and Twycross [Leics.]. A radio network for Home Defence, police, fire and ROC use was also maintained through Hill-top Radio Stations. In Sub-Regions 31 and 32, there were stations, recorded in War Plan UK, at: SR31 Idle, Robin Hood's Hills, Kirkby-in-Ashfield, Alport Height, Sir William Hill, Hutchinson's Holt, Kirkby Underwood, Normanby-le-Wold, Grange Farm, Fulnetby, Stanston [depot] SR32 Potcote, Old Poor's Gorse, Bardon Hill, Glebe Farm.

Several of these site are shared by both Hill-top and Microwave facilities. Copt Oak/Bardon Hill [Leics.] and Kirkby Underwood [Lincs.] for instance. Also must be noted, here, RAF Digby [Lincs.] the RAF/GCHQ listening station, and the Army's equivalent station, at Garrat's Hay [Leics.]. Outside Crowland [Lincs.] is the mast and equipment huts of a former USAF radio-relay station, in use 1961-79. It was one of a network which included masts at Kirton-in-Lindsey, and Spitalgate. The more up-to-date RAF Croughton [Northants.], used by the USAF as a signals station, has a fine array of masts, dishes and golf-balls. Many of the installations still have military, civil, commercial or domestic purposes. One must be thankful, most were never required to fulfil their original functions.

8 BARRACKS, CAMPS, EXPLOSIVES STORES & DEPOTS

The archetypal structure of the twentieth century military landscape is the hutted camp. These were built for a wide variety of purposes ranging from accommodation for the complements of Coast Defence or Anti-aircraft batteries, to prisoner-of-war camps. The sudden and rapid expansion of the armed forces on the outbreak of war necessitated an immediate solution to the problem of supplementing the permanent barracks of the peace-time regular forces, and the established drill halls of the part-time territorials and reserves. As well as accommodating vast increases in personnel, similarly significant increases in materiel had to be housed. Prior to the outbreak of World War II, a network of mobilisation centres was established, to hold weapons and equipment, to be issued to newly-raised units. These worked in tandem with the established munitions stores and Royal Ordnance Factories. This chapter examines the range of structures within these related headings.

EXPLOSIVES FACTORIES AND STORES AND MOBILISATION DEPOTS

The particular type of warfare developed in the trenches of World War I, created an insatiable demand for explosives, especially shells. Existing gunpowder factories such as Fernilee [Derbys.], active from 1801, could not meet demand, so new ones were built. At Chilwell, Viscount Chetwynd, recruited by Lloyd George to bring a fresh approach to the problem of under-production, designed his shell-filling plant in 1915. Using existing, transferable technology for processes such as milling and grinding, in a converted silk mill, his task was to turn 1000 tons of high explosive into shells every week. Building materials were diverted from other projects, and, before the end of the War, he had constructed a vast underground shell store, the only one in the country, which held nearly a million filled shells. These would be taken by railway to Army Ordnance Department stores such as Weedon Bec [Northants.] prior to being issued to units. Weedon also dated from the Napoleonic Wars, when it had been established, on the Grand Union Canal, as a strategically-placed arms depot, barracks, and royal bolt-hole in case of invasion. Much of the site still remains as warehousing. Chilwell was National Filling Factory No.6. Another, NFF No.9, was at Banbury Warkworth [Northants.]. Only in operation from 1916-24, its site now lies adjacent to the M40. It was commissioned as the first war-production Lyddite factory and was locally designed. As well as filling shells with explosive, there was some, limited, work on filling shells with gas. The Office of Works, in 1917, designed the purpose-built mine-filling factory at Gainsborough [Lincs.] for the Royal Navy, whose output was probably then transported by rail to the RN Mines Depot at nearby Haxey, still in use in World War II. Much ingenuity was applied to adapting by-products of established industries to munitions. Cotton-waste from mills in Whaley Bridge, Charlesworth and Lee Valley [Derbys.], and from Ley's, Canterbury Road Mill, Old Radford [Notts], was used in the manufacture of gun-cotton. Anglo Shirley Aldred & Co. of Worksop [Notts.] produced acetate of lime at their wood chemical plant. At Langwith [Derbys.], HM Factory processing ammonium perchlorate for explosives production, was located next to the colliery whose output included the appropriate by-products. Here, workers' housing, both family homes and hostels, as well as grander residences for the management, were provided, and still stand. Explosives production was a dangerous business, and at Chilwell, in July 1918, 134 workers were killed in an accidental TNT-related explosion. The dangers continued after hostilities ceased, five workers dying in accidents at Banbury, Warkworth, processing surplus and outdated ordnance.

By the mid-1930s, it had become apparent that another European war was likely. In order to facilitate mobilisation, specialised depots were established across the country to stockpile equipment, especially anti-aircraft weaponry, ready for issuing to the new Territorial Army units being raised and trained to counter the expected bomber offensive. A number of RAOC depots were built around Nottingham, at Bestwood Lodge, Arnold, now rebuilt as a Police HQ, and Bulwell. A REME depot beside the A1 at Newark [Notts.] is now a motor-caravan dealership, and only one or two original buildings remain. Many of these Mobilisation Centres were built to a standard pattern, an example of which can be seen outside Oundle [Northants]. It consists of a large high-roofed vehicle storage shed, workshops, guardhouse, garages, caretaker's bungalow etc. all built in brick, in a style similar to that used for Expansion Period RAF airfields. Other stores, were to other designs, and an example can be seen on the old A1, north of Grantham [Lincs.l. This consists of a range of A-Frame sheds. Chilwell and Derby were Central Ordnance Depots, with out-stations all around. The depot at Old Dalby [Leics.] was established in 1939, for vehicle storage, but soon took on an enhanced role, not only storing, but building, repairing, and maintaining vehicles, machinery and equipments, employing 4000 military and civilian operatives. In 1942, REME was formed, and Old Dalby's functions have continued to increase in scale and complexity ever since. Many original buildings still stand, along with those from later periods. The RAF had a Stores and Ordnance Depot at Basford [Notts.] served by a private siding.

Chilwell's role as a Royal Ordnance Factory may have changed, but new ROFs were built, such as that at Kings Meadow, Nottingham. Ranskill [Notts.] was the last cordite factory to be built in World War II. Most of it has now been demolished and landscaped, but the odd industrial building and some workers' houses survive. Filling Factories No. 10 at Queniborough [Leics.], for fuses and detonators, and No. 14 at Ruddington [Notts], for bombs up to 1 000 lb, were in operation throughout most of the war, but FF No.20, planned for Northampton, was never built. The World War 1 proofing range at Asfordby [Leics.] was re-activated for further service. The administration site of the explosives depot at Yardley Chase [Northants.] still stands, used by army cadets, and as an outdoor education centre. In 1942, the disused railway tunnel at Rowthorne [Notts.] was pressed into temporary service as a Forward Ammunition Depot.

The East Midlands formed a significant part of the vast concentration of bomber bases, and, therefore, housed many of the bomb dumps, known to the RAF as Maintenance Units [MUs], and to the USAAF as Ordnance Depots. Norton Disney [Lincs], housed 93MU, a Forward Ammunition Depot, whilst 100MU was at South Witham [Lincs.]. Their capacity for safe storage was 15 and 10 Kilotons of high explosive, respectively. These amounts, often representing their weekly turnover, arrived direct from the explosives factories, and were quickly moved into storage on their neighbouring airfields, prior to use. The USAAF had ordnance depots at Braybrooke [Northants], and at Sudbury [Derbys]. Other US central quarter-master stores were at Kettering, Thrapston, Wellingborough [Northants], and in Leicester.

The remains of a number of temporary military depots from the World War II period can still be seen in our area. Boughton [Notts.], now an industrial estate, is still recognisable as a supply depot, with its rows of Romney huts. At Saxondale [Notts.] the guardroom, office, and two large, brick-built, gabled double store-houses survive from the Army Storage Depot, used by the Royal Engineers. At Bottesford [Notts.] No. 17 Army Fuel Depot, along with the associated RASC camp, consisted of dozens of Nissen huts, underground water-storage tanks, and fuel-tanks sited on low mounds of sand. The extensive site was served by narrow-gauge railway, which linked into the sidings which, in turn, connected to Bottesford West Junction. Fuel, in jerry cans manufactured by Raleigh Cycles of Nottingham, was moved around by men of the Royal Pioneer Corps. Neighbouring Whatton Camp, now a prison, provided some services, but the depot was, for the most part, self-sufficient, with its own cinema, NAAFFI, officers' mess etc. Decoy fires gave the site some protection from bombing, and strict security on the ground deterred potential saboteurs. It was, nevertheless, claimed as a successful target by Lord Haw-Haw. Other fuel depots were at Stow [Lincs.], with structures from World War II still sited alongside the railway, and at Redmile [Leics]. The RASC also had a depot at Winthorpe Hall, near Newark [Notts.]. The Royal Engineers had a searchlight depot at Fulney Park, Spalding [Lincs.]. Rushton Hall [Northants.] was a RAOC officer training unit, and Billing Hall [Northants.] an army transport depot, base for Czech troops, and AA training centre. The RE Northern Command Post at Canwick, was converted into a modern house, known locally as Canwick Cathedral, by Sam Scorer in the 1970s.

Other large camps were at Clumber Park, used for transit of troops, tank-training, and for ammunition storage; Orston, Kneeton, Bowbridge Road and Hawton, [Notts]. Some camps were associated with specific units or operations. In World War I, the Machine-gun Corps was raised at Belton House [Lincs.] mainly from a nucleus of hitherto-horsed Yeomanry cavalry, brought back from Palestine in 1915. There was a large, hutted army camp at Clipstone [Notts.] in World War I. In World War II, the RAF Regiment was founded at Alma Park, Grantham, in 1942, soon moving to Belton. Prior to the airborne operations of 1944, many of the troops involved were housed and trained in camps at Ashwell, Braunstone Park, where the US 82nd Airborne Division was based, and Scraptoft [Leics.], convenient for the airfields of the Ninth USAAF, who would deliver them to the Continent. Fulbeck Hall [Lincs.] was the HQ of 1st Airborne Division, which also occupied Harlaxton Manor [Lincs.]. Ashwell is now a prison, Harlaxton an American university, and Fulbeck is often open to the public, displaying Arnhem memorabilia in the very rooms in which the operation was planned. Village halls around the area contain graffiti relating to the units and their operations ahead. During World War II, the Royal Navy took over Butlin's holiday camp, outside Skegness [Lincs.], as HMS Royal Arthur, a basic training facility. A little way up the coast at Trusthorpe, is a former army camp, whose huts are now used as holiday chalets.

BARRACKS AND DRILL HALLS

In 1914, many of the reservists and Territorials were mobilised at the old regimental depots built around 1880 when the Cardwell reforms localised the regular infantry, the barracks at Lincoln, Glen Plarva [Leics.], Normanton [Derbys.], Northampton and Nottingham. Whilst nothing survives at Nottingham, and only the gate-piers at Derby, and one barrack-block at Northampton, much of Glen Parva remains, as does the pseudo-mediaeval keep and gatehouse at Sobraon Barracks, Lincoln. From an even earlier period are the militia barracks at Lincoln and Grantham [Lincs.], Clare Street, Northampton, and Rowditch Barracks, Derby. Territorials in Leicester, joined up in 1914, at the drill hall complex centred around the fifteenth century Magazine Gateway, still to be seen on an island in the Ring Road. The period between the establishment of the Territorial Force in 1908, and the outbreak of war in 1914, however, saw a busy programme of drill hall construction. Hinckley, Melton Mowbray and Shepshed [Leics]; Church Gresley and Ilkeston [Derbys]; Boston, Spalding and Stamford [Lincs.]; Oakham [Rutland]; Oundle [Northants.]; and Newark and Southwell [Notts.] all date from this time.

Re-armament during the 1930s necessitated a total re-think of the role of the new Territorial Army, reconstituted in 1920. If war were to come, then it would come to Britain from the air, and this notion was confirmed by events in Spain. The TA was re-organised to take on an anti-aircraft role. Many infantry and Yeomanry cavalry units were assigned to the Royal Engineers as searchlight batteries, or to the Royal Artillery as gunners. The new drill hall in Newport, Lincoln, proudly bears the old badge of the Tenth Foot, with its Egyptian sphinx, but, below, is a new inscription'. "46 [Lincolnshire] AA Battalion". The old Victorian drill halls had looked like forts; the pre-1914 drill halls looked like gentlemen's residences-, now, they were to be, either neo-Georgian, to suggest a connection with the new RAF stations, or art deco, to resemble the new technology-based factories from which the TA wished to recruit its skilled workers. Particularly fine examples of such buildings can be seen at Newark, Retford [Notts.]. Blackbird Road, Ulverscroft Road and Brentwood Road, Leicester; Frodingham and Westward Ho, Grimsby [Lincs.]; and Kingsway, Derby, whose 1939 date stone reads: "just in time". The former TA Centre at Eckington [Derbys.] is replicated in Alfreton by the barracks of 9 Training Battalion RASC, in operation throughout World War II. In both World Wars, Northampton Racecourse had hosted a hutted camp, mainly for use as an extra regimental depot. In 1941, the Northamptonshire Regiment got its new depot, Quebec Barracks, at Wootton. This later became the Royal Pioneer Corps depot, and has only recently been demolished. During World War II, a number of stately homes were requisitioned as barracks. These included Coleorton Hall [Leics.]; Markeaton and Egginton Halls [Derbys.]; Haselbech Hall, home to the 11 Bn. Worcestershire Regiment, Ashby St Legers, base for 6 Bn. Leicestershire Regiment, Deene Park, Finedon Hall, where Free French troops were based, and Castle Ashby [Northants.].

PRISONER-OF-WAR CAMPS

The eighteenth century Gothic Donington Hall [Leics.] was only one of dozens of World War I PoW camps in our region. Photographs show it with 9-foot-high barbed-wire fences and watch-towers, guarded by veterans of the Leicestershire Regiment with fixed bayonets, but, despite all this,

PINGLEY CAMP [Lincs.]. This PoW Camp near Brigg retains most of its original features and layout; TA018168.

successful escapes were made. Nicol lists over 100 camps and work-gangs in the East Midlands. These include Ragdale Hall and Loughborough Workhouse [Leics.]; Somerby Hall and Boston Docks [Lines.]; Ranskill, Tuxford and Retford depots [Notts.]; Oakwell Colliery and Kilburn Hall [Derbys.], and Guilsborough Grammar School and Upton Vicarage [Northants].

World War II would appear to present a far less eclectic approach. Most PoW camps now occupied green-field sites, and were built to a common layout, using common building designs. They were divided into two main compounds, one administrative, with offices, workshops, guardroom, water-tower, guards' quarters, detention block, etc; the other containing the prisoners' living accommodation, ablutions, messes, and recreation facilities. Virtually the entire layout can be seen at Pingley Camp near Brigg, and significant elements at Moorby, Low Fulney and Potterhanworth [Lincs.]; Caunton, near Southwell, and Headon, near Retford [Notts.]. Some big houses were, however, used, Swanwick [Derbys.] being the first camp for interned Nazis. After the end of World War II, many former airfields were pressed into service to house PoWs. Camp No. 16, Kingscliffe [Northants.] was a distribution centre, passing prisoners on to other camps such as Woolfox Lodge [Rutland]. Many of the decaying buildings of these camps contain grafitti, or, as at Caunton, painted panels of landscape scenes back home.

• Many of the structures detailed in this chapter were designed only to fast a short while. Others were temporary adaptations of domestic or commercial buildings. For whatever explanation, the end result is that very little remains to be seen. It is thus especially important that a memory of short-lived, but nevertheless significant, military activity is recorded and retained.

9 WAR SUPPLIES IN TWO WORLD WARS

The escalation of military technology of the late nineteenth century was a product of industrialisation, and so it was to Industry that the military turned for solutions to the problems of the battlefield. We have already seen how peacetime industries approached the production of bombs and shells. Now we will see how, to some extent in World War I, and to a much greater degree in World War 11, the whole economy responded to the insatiable appetite of the war-machine, and of those, civilian or military, who had little choice but to service it.

MUNITIONS PRODUCTION IN WORLD WAR I

Many firms switched their normal output from peacetime products to wartime ones, often building machines designed by other firms. Ruston Proctor & Co Ltd, of Lincoln, built more aero engines than any other manufacturer, and also constructed over 2000 aircraft, including 1600 Sopwith Camels. It was one of their BE2 aircraft which shot down the first Zeppelin to be destroyed in British airspace. In other parts of the city, Robey's built Sopwith Gunbuses and Short 184 Seaplanes, whilst Clayton & Shuttleworth initially made parts for aircraft, but graduated to building Sopwith Triplanes and Camels. The aircraft acceptance park at Bracebridge Heath, just outside Lincoln, was set up by Robey's in 1916, and used by other companies as well. Later, the Royal Flying Corps constructed the General Service, or Belfast Truss hangars for their Handley-Page bombers. Demolition has recently taken place at this important site, but the Aircraft Repair Shed, now a car show-room, remains in good order. Marshall's of Gainsborough [Lincs.] built 150 Bristol F2B reconnaissance aircraft.

OUNDLE [Northants.]. Mobilisation Centre, c1935, built to store AA guns, vehicles and other equipment for issue to TA and new units on the outbreak of hostilities; similar buildings were at Chilwell and Bulwell [Notts.]; TL043858.

Probably the most memorable contribution to the war effort came from Foster of Lincoln. Between July and December 1915, Colonel Ernest Swinton, William Tritton, Foster's managing director, and Lieutenant WG Wilson, developed an armoured tractor with caterpillar tracks. Little Willie, the prototype, impressed the military in trials in Clumber Park [Notts.] and so Foster's proceeded with a production model which went into action in 1916, during the final stages of the battle of the Somme. Some 2500 tanks were built by the end of the War, many of which were built at Foster's works. Tritton was also involved in the development of the faster Whippet tank,and Foster's received an order for 400 of these in 1917. Marshall of Gainsborough built unarmed tanks for delivering supplies to the frontline. Foster also constructed 12 inch howitzers. In addition to aircraft, Rustons produced 8000 Lewis machine-guns, and Robey made cordite presses, mines, generator sets and depth charges. Hornsby of Grantham made gun-mountings, HE shell-casings, and marine engines. Blackstone's of Stamford [Lincs.] produced machinery for submarines, and spare parts for naval motor-boats. The British United Shoe Machinery Co. of Leicester, made high-angle anti-aircraft Pom-pom guns. Brush Electrical Engineering, at their Falcon Works in Loughborough [Leics.] built nearly 100 Maurice Farman timber S7 Longhorns for the Admiralty, and then a few of its metal successor, the Henri Farman Astral. They also produced over 500 Avro 504s of various marks, and Short 827 and 184 Seaplanes in significant quantities. Normal aircraft were flown out, having been tested on the adjacent Meadows, but the Short seaplanes had to be dismantled and sent off by rail. Rolls-Royce had been established in Derby since 1906, and, in 1914, they were approached by the Admiralty to build Renault aero engines, but felt they could come up with something better themselves. The 225hp Eagle engine was developed, followed by the Falcon and the Hawk. By the end of the War, 60% of all aero engines were supplied by Rolls-Royce, for use in a wide range of aircraft. The traditional industries of the region: coal and power, mineral extraction, textiles, boots and shoes, chemical refinement, pharmaceuticals, timber, tobacco, food production and processing etc. were all eventually geared to War production.

MUNITIONS PRODUCTION IN WORLD WAR II

In 1934, Rolls-Royce had set up an aero engine test-flying centre at RAF Hucknall [Notts.], where they developed the PV-12, or Merlin engine. On the outbreak of war, all vehicle production was shifted to their Crewe works, leaving Derby exclusively for aero engine manufacture. Late in the War, testing of jet engines was carried out at RAF Church Broughton [Derbys.]. Other local firms particularly heavily involved in weapons manufacture were British Celanese [later Courtaulds] and Qualcast. Brush Coachworks at Loughborough were, once again, in the forefront of aircraft production. At first they were involved in the all-timber Bristol, later Armstrong-Whitworth Albemarle. On the removal of this line to Gloucestershire, Brush sub-contracted for the repair of Handley Page Hampdens from the Derby LMS Locomotive Works, and built parts for Lancasters. From early in 1944, they then built nearly 500 deHavilland Dorninies. These were flown out from their new airfield on the Derby

SHEPSHED [Leics.]. Drill Hall on Kings Road, 1914. This imposing neo-Baroque building, was home to G Coy. 5Bn. Leicestershire Regt. Territorial Force; similar buildings remain in Melton Mowbray, Oakham, & Hinckley; SK477185.

Road, formerly the Racecourse, and now buried under an industrial estate. At Sywell [Northants.] Brooklands Aviation opened a plant in 1940 for overhauling Wellington bombers, nearly 2000 passing through during the War. Some were converted to transports. There was also an Armstrong Whitworth factory, on site, assembling Whitleys, Manchesters, and, from 1943, Lancaster IIs. Most of the Ministry of Aircraft Production hangars remain. Two large double A Frame sheds, a Bellman, and two side-opening sheds, all used by Brooklands still stand, as do two T2-type hangars used by Armstrong-Whitworth, along with most of the factory's ancillary buildings, many integral with the Flying Training Schools, which operated alongside. The Brooklands work with Vickers Wellinqtons was only part of an extensive operation which was centred on purpose-built premises at Buttocks Booth, Northampton, and used dispersed sites, mainly requisitioned garages around the area. The Armstrong Whitworth work on Lancasters involved use of the Corporation Tram Depot in Northampton for assembly, and the manufac-

81-2 DERBY. TA Centre, Kingsway, 1939, this neo-Georgian building was intended as HQ of the new 2 AA Div. being raised from 1937 to defend the Midlands against bombing raids, throughout the War it was HQ of the AA Bde. which defended Derby and Nottingham; SK733346.

CHILWELL [Notts.]. The derelict sheds of the former Royal Ordnance Factory which produced munitions through two world wars; demolition was well under way in Spring 2003, following its closure the previous year; SK514354.

ture of a whole range of components at nearby factories, including Express Lifts, and, from the shoe trade, Manfields, Barratts and The Cantilever Shoe Co. At RAF Hucknall, Rolls-Royce occupied two of the four 1916 Coupled GS sheds, and other buildings. Theirs have gone, but the other two sheds still stand, off Watnall Road. RAF Tollerton [Notts.] provided a base for Field Services Ltd. who employed 700 people in the repair and overhaul of a variety of bomber aircraft, mainly Lancasters. Work was also undertaken, earlier in the War, to re-assemble and fly Hampdens, which had been repaired at Loughborough. From late in 1943, RAF Bitteswell [Leics.], now Magna Park Distribution Centre, was used by Armstrong Whitworth to test fly Lancasters from their Northamptonshire workshops. Boulton & Paul assembled Horsa gliders at their plant on King Street, Melton Mowbray [Leics]. Taylorcraft built the Auster, army co-operation aircraft at their plant at Rearsby throughout the War. Aircraft production finally ceased here in 1964, and the buildings were taken over by British Leyland.

As well as aircraft there was a need for a vast range of war materials for use on land and at sea. In Derby, Alton's Foundry produced pipework for warships, while Crompton Parkinson was making degaussing cable for merchant ships. The LMS Works produced rolling stock, hospital trains, tank turrets, and reconditioned 23 World War I rail-mounted 12 inch howitzers. They also manufactured optical equipment such as gun-sights. Bliss, opened in 1940, produced shell-casings, and Ley's Malleable Mouldings, became a target for Luftwaffe bombs. The Express Lift Co. in Northampton ran a number of operations, including the production of 7.2", 6", 5.5", and 4.5" shells. In Lincoln, the now amalgamated, Ruston and Hornsby, built hundreds of tanks and armoured gun-tractors, as well as diesel engines for every conceivable application from locos and boats, to generators for search-lights. Robey made main propulsion engines for corvettes and frigates, and Smith Clayton Forge, crankshafts for aero engines. The excavating division of Ruston and Hornsby, had, in 1930, joined up with Bucyrus-Erie of Milwaukee, USA. In 1939, Churchill, at the time, First Lord of the Admiralty, asked the firm to produce a trench-cutting machine. Ruston-Bucyrus duly came up with Nellie, who performed well in trials at Skellingthorpe [Lincs.] and, later, in front of its commissioner, at Clumber Park. However, this war was to be different from the previous one, and the 140 ton Nellie proved unnecessary. in Grantham [Lincs.] Ruston and Hornsby made naval equipment, Aveling-Barford built Bren-gun carriers and tanks, and British MARCO produced Hispano-Suiza and Oerlikon LAA guns, mainly for the Navy. Next door to them, in Springfield Road, was a MAP factory. There were shadow factories for British MARCO at Hungerton Hall and Stoke Rochford Hall. Here parallel production could be maintained, with a total transfer of production were the main factory to be destroyed by bombing. Hungerton Hall retains the buildings erected for this purpose. In Gainsborough, Marshalls made anti-tank and LAA guns, naval gun-mountings, and, in 1942, midget submarines. Rose Brothers made precision instruments such as gun-sights and predictors for anti-aircraft use. In Scunthorpe [Lincs.] Appleby-Frodingham produced steel plate, applying it to extemporised armoured vehicles at first, and then as needs changed,

REARSBY [Leics.]. The former Taylorcraft aircraft factory whose most famous product was the Auster army co-operation aircraft; SK658136.

to landing-craft for the invasion of France. Stewart and Lloyd's Corby [Northants.] steelworks was one of the biggest in the country. It mobilised its resources to produce the 1000 miles of pipeline for the Hamel element of PLUTO, in 20′ and 40′ lengths. In Newark [Notts.] RHP made ball-bearings for use in Rolls-Royce Merlin aero engines, and British Timken of Duston [Northants.] made roller-bearings. This was a shadow factory, whose value was quickly demonstrated when the parent factory, in Birmingham, was bombed out. Bassett-Lowke of Northampton, the famous model railway makers, produced models of various projects including the Bailey Bridge, and the Mulberry Harbour caissons, as well as simulators for AA training. As well as new work in aviation and weapons manufacture, Northamptonshire's shoe factories still needed to maintain their traditional output. However, here there were also new demands. Haynes & Cann Ltd. produced a flying boot consisting of a normal civilian shoe with a detachable sheepskin upper. Concealed in the heel was a compass, for evasion, and maps, invisibly printed on silk, were inserted in the leg. Gas used for Barrage Balloons, passed through the Air Ministry Gas Cylinder Testing Station at Wellingborough

Gas Works [Northants.] Wicksteed of Kettering [Northants.] made sawing equipment for industrial and Armed Forces use. Something of the complexity of weapons production can be seen simply by looking at the manufacture of the army's staple- the 0.303" SMLE rifle. Whilst the major undertaking of producing 25000 rifles a month throughout the War, was essentially the role of certain Royal Ordnance Factories, many of the parts, and some up- grading of older models to Weedon Repair Standard, was sub-contracted to dozens of small, private companies, mainly in the Midlands, and in London. The companies involved in such work in our region are shown below:

ILBerridge & Co Ltd; Leicester: magazine catches
British United Shoe Machinery Co; Leicester:stockbolts; and for spare parts for up-grading Mk 1 rifles. back sight beds, triggers, keeper plates
Dean Bros.;Nottingham:magazine cases, springs
Hanwell Engineering Co;Northampton:boltheads
Premier Screw & Repetition Co; Leicester:screws, pins, rivets
ATRalphs;Leicester: strikers, pins, + Mkl strikers
Standard Rotary Machine Co; Rushden: magazine catches
Timson Bullock Barber Ltd; Kettering: backsight beds
Gimson & Co Vulcan Road; Leicester:triggers
Herberts Ltd Chelsea St.; Nottingharn: sears, extractor springs, sear springs, sling swivels
Job Lee, Premier Engineering; Kettering:cocking pieces
Messrs Wildt & Co; Leicester: extractors
General Presswork & Stampings; Leicester: buttplates, brackets, swivels
North Bridge Engineering; Leicester: stockbolts, collars, screws
BSA Factory; Mansfield: parts for Mk 1

Whilst manufacturing was important, so was the supply of natural raw materials. The gypsum mines around Bunny, south of Nottingham, the lime and iron-stone quarries and the cement works of north-east Northamptonshire and east Leicestershire, were all vital to the war effort. In 1943, drill-ing specialists from the USA, were billeted with the monks

BOUGHTON [Notts.]. Some of the rows and rows of Romney huts of this supply depot, now private businesses; SK684680.

of Kelham Theological College, in order to work the Eakring [Notts.] oil-field. They raised significant quantities of oil, throughout the remainder of the War. At Denby [Derbys.] the Ministry of Supply had a grit factory.

The contribution to the nation's foodstocks of local agriculture, must not be forgotten. Girls of the Land Army, along with many prisoners-of-war, worked with the farmers to produce the food, using both traditional methods, and new techniques, based on machinery built in the local engineering works of Lincoln, Nottingham and Derby. New food-processing methods were necessary to avoid waste. In Spalding [Lincs.] new canning plants were set up, and in Boston [Lincs.] a potato-drying plant started up. Food-stocks were stored by the Ministry of Food at Belper [Derbys.] Buffer Depot No. 38. at Newstead Abbey [Notts.]; at Shepshed [Leics.]. and at the Ministry Cold Stores at Sutton-in-Ashfield [Notts], Loughborough [Leics.], and at many other places. In some areas, Land-girls lived communally in specially-built hostels, some examples of which remain. Some hostels were in converted existing buildings such as the village hall, as at Leverton [Lincs.].

SITE GAZETTEER

Notes

1 This is a list only of examples, surviving at time of compilation, not a full inventory.

2 Where NGRs are given, they are 6 figure, and therefore only approximate.

3 Drawing numbers, shown in certain chapters, show sequence/ year of production. Thus the Watch Office for all Commands was built to the 343rd design to emerge from the Air Ministry drawing office in 1943 hence 343/43.

AIRFIELD BUILDINGS [Chapter 1]

Watch-offices and Control Towers

Duty pilot's office: single-storey brick hut, Tydd St Mary, Lincs.

Watch-office with tower [FORT type] **1959/34** & **207/36**, Digby, Lincs.

as above, tower removed, and later extension to side,Hemswell, Lincs.

Watch-office [experimental, only one other built] **756/36**, Manby, Lincs.

Watch-office with met. section [VILLA type **2328/39**, Waddington, Lincs.

as above, but in brick not concrete **5845/39**, Swinderby, Lincs. also Newton and Syerston, Notts. and North Luffenham, [Rutland]

Watch-office with Met section, temp. brick, **518/40**, Bottesford, Leics. also Goxhill, Lincs. and Wymeswold, Leics.

Watch-office for Night-fighters, **12096/41**, Kingscliffe, Northants. also Coleby Grange and Hibaldstow, Lincs.

Watch office & ops room for Bomber satellites Type A **13079/41** Langar, Notts.

as above for Bomber satellites Type B **7345/41** & **4170/43** Waltham, Lincs.

Watch-office for Bomber & OTU satellites, **13726/41**, Gamston, Notts. also Bardney, Lincs.

Watch-office for all commands, **343/43**, Leicester East, Leics. also Ashbourne, Derbys; Barkston Heath, East Kirkby, Sandtoft, Sturgate, and Wickenby, Lincs, Bruntingthorpe and Husbands Bosworth, Leics; Silverstone, Northants; that at Strubby, Lincs., has an added VCR .

Unclassified design with no known drawing number Wigstey, Notts.

Control Tower, vertical split, **2548c/55**, Scampton, Lincs.

Local Control Tower, side-by-side, **7378a/S5**, Swinderby, Lincs.

Visual Control Room [VCR] **5871c/5 5,** North Luffenham, Rutand

Hangars

RFC Aircraft Repair Shed, **164/17**, Bracebridge Heath, Lincs.
RFC Coupled General Service Sheds, **332/17**, Hucknall, Notts.
Type F Shed, side opening, **1947/27**, Sutton Bridge, Lincs. also in use by Brooklands Aviation for aircraft assembly at Sywell, Northants, a version with a double gable stands at North Coates, Lincs.
Bellman Hangar, **8349/37**, North Coates, Lincs. also at Hucknall, Notts.
Hipped C Aircraft Repair Shed, **9106/36**, Manby, Lincs.
Hipped C Hangar, **4292/35**, Manby, Lincs. also at Cottesmore, Rutland, Digby & Hemswell, Lincs.
Austerity C Hangar, **8180/38** & **5533/39**, Binbrook, Lincs. also Newton, Notts;
J Type Hangar, **5836/39**, Chipping Warden, Northants. also Polebrook, Northants. Elsham Wolds, Goxhill, & Swinderby, Lincs. Syerston, Notts, North Lufenham, Rutiand.,
T2 Hangar, **8254/40**, Desborough, Northants. also Bardney, Barkston Heath, Lines, Bottesford, Leics. Ashbourne, Derbys;
B1 Hangar, **11776/41**, Church Broughton, Derbys. also Coningsby, Faldingworth, Spilsby, Strubby & Wickenby, Lincs.
Miskins Blister Hangar, **12497/41**, Caistor, Lincs. also Sywell, Northants. Wickenby, Lincs, [steel] & Hucknall, Notts. [timber]
Gaydon Hangar, **7527/55**, Coningsby, Lincs.

Domestic site buildings

Officers Mess, 3-storey, **3935/35**, Manby, Lincs.
Officers Mess, 2-storey with wings, **570-2/37**, Swinderby, Lincs. also Newton, Notts, Hemswell, Lincs.
Sergeants Mess, 2-storey; **11527/38** & **14557/39** Newton, Notts. also Swinderby, Lincs.
Barrack Block Type J, 3-storey, **74/35**, Manby, Lincs.
Barrack Block Type B, 3-storey, **177/35**, Manby, Lincs.
Barrack Block, 2-storey, flat roof, **1132/38**, Newton, Notts.
Barrack Block, 2-storey, hipped roof, **11587/38**, Waddington, Lincs.
Officers' married quarters, **528/39**, Langtoft, Lincs.
Station Sick Quarters, **1963/34**, Manby, Lincs.
Station Sick Quarters, **7503-4/37**, Swinderby, Lincs.
Station Sick Quarters + Decontamination Centre, Newton, Notts.

Administrative buildings

Guardhouse & Post Office, **1621/27**, Hucknall, Notts.
Guardhouse, **4534/35**, Manby, Lincs.

Guardhouse with Fire Party, **469/38**, Hemswell, Lincs.
Guardhouse in temporary brick, **222/40**, Strubby, Lincs.
Picket Post, **14294/40**, Ingham, Lincs.
Station HQ, **1723/36**, Waddington, Lincs.
Station HQ with Ops. Block, **1723/36**, Hemswell, Lincs.
Station HQ, **190/36**, Manby, Lincs.
Station Office in temporary brick, ?, Bruntingthorpe, Leics.
Operations Block in temporary brick, **5586/40**, Bottesford, Leics.
Operations Block in temporary brick, **228/43**, Harrington, Northants.
Speech Broadcast Building, **10786/41**, Bruntingthorpe, Leics.
PBX, Telephone Exchange, **5648/41**, Kingscliffe, Northants.
Gymnasium, **16428/40**, Desborough, Northants.
Gymnasium & Church, **15424/41**, Metheringham, Lincs.
Gymnasium & Cinema, **889/42**, Goxhill, Lincs.
Squash Court, **16589/40**, Metheringham, Lincs.
Blast shelter, open/surface, Bottesford, Leics., & Ashbourne, Derbys.
Stanton shelter, Wigsley, Notts. & Metheringham, Lincs.
Surface shelters for 50 persons, some strengthened for LAA; Kingscliffe, Northants.

Training buildings
Station Education Centre, **3702/35**, Manby, Lincs.
Instructional Block, **3217/36**, Manby, Lincs.
Link Trainer Building, **12386/38**, Newton, Notts.
Link Trainer Hut in temporary brick, **4188/42**, Deenethorpe, Northants.
Air Ministry Laboratory Bombing Teacher **47/40**
Double AML Bombing Teacher, **6301/42**, Melton Mowbray, Leics
Triple AML Bombing Teacher, **1739/41**, Silverstone, Northants.
Combined Bombing teacher & Turret trainer [now house], Darley Moor, Derbys.
Turret Instructional Building, **11023/40**, Metheringham, Lincs.
Double Turret Instructional Building, **11023/40**, Silverstone, Northants.
Turret Instructional + AML Bombing Teacher **936-7/43**, Woolfox Lodge, Rutland
Free gunnery trainer, Blister hangar, Waltham [Grimsby], Lincs.
Fisher Gunnery Trainer, **10839/42**, Bruntingthorpe, Leics.
Synthetic Navigation Trainer, **2075/43**, Strubby, Lincs.
non-standard synthetictraining building, ?, Sandtoft, Lincs.

Technical site buildings
Fuel Tanker Shed 4-bay, **2773/34**, Newton, Notts.
Night Flying Equipment [NFE] Store, **3235/39**, Hemswell, Lincs.

NFE Store in temporary brick, **12411/41**, Bottesford, Leics.
Fire-engine shed in temporary brick, **12563/40**, Husbands Bosworth, Leics.
Dinghy Store, **2901/43**, Ingham, Lincs.
Gas Respirator Store, **13730/41**, Ingham, Lincs.
Parachute store, **1971/34**, Manby & Waddington, Lincs.
Parachute store, **175/36**, Newton, Notts. & Binbrook, Lincs.
Parachute store, **11137/41**, Wymeswold, Leics.
Parachute store, **10825/42**, Gamston, Notts.
Main stores, **808/27**, Hucknall, Notts.
Main stores, **2057/34**, Manby & Waddington, Lincs.
Main stores, **7064/37**, Swinderby, Lincs. & Newton, Notts.
Main stores, **1256/40**, Goxhill, Lincs.
Main stores, Romney huts, Keistern, Lincs.
Armoury/store, **2233/34**, Hucknall, Notts.
Armoury/photo', in concrete, **4829/35**, Cottesmore, Rutiand &Hemswell, Lincs.
Armoury/photo', in brick, **7616/37**, Swinderby, Lincs.
Station workshops, **6957/37**, Binbrook, Lincs.
Station workshops, Romney huts, Spanhoe, Northants.
Station workshops in temporary brick **12774/41**, Bottesford, Leics.
Water tower, brick encased, **957/38**, Binbrook, Hemswell & Manby, Lincs.
Water-tower, single Braithwaite tank on steel lattice, Metheringham, Lincs.
Water-tower, as above but double tanks, Swinderby, Lincs.

Hutting

- MOWP standard hut East Kirkby, Lincs.
- 24'span Nissen hut, Bottesford, Leics.
- 16" span Nissen hut East Kirkby, Lincs.
- Marston hut Bottestord, Leics.
- Seco hutting Fiskerton ROC HQ, Lincs.
- Romney &/or Iris huts Desborough, Northants.
- Handeraft hut Harlaxton, Lines.
- Laing hut Waltharn [Grimsby], Lines.
- Sectional timber hutting North Coates, Lines.

Range structures

Grimsthorpe Park, Lincs. Quadrant Tower: TF031205
Preston Capes, Northants. Quadrant Tower: SP592550
Holbeach St Matthew, bombing range buildings: TF4432
Wainfleet Sands, control tower of weapons range: TF522570

Other RAF sites

Grantham, St Vincents, Lines, HQ 5 Group Bomber Command. SK926350

Nocton Hall, Lincs. military hospital in WWII; used by RAF until 1983. TF062643

Rauceby, Lincs. RAF hospital 1940-47: TF042441

Tattershall Thorpe, Lincs: radio station in use up to 1981: TF226591

COAST DEFENCE [Chapter 2]

Haile Sand FortTA349062;Stailingborough Bty[fragments] TA222147

Tetney Haven [OP + pillbox] TA352031/354030

Horseshoe Point [OP + blockhouse] TA381018

Pyes Hall [6pdr. gunhouse, 2 pillboxes, blockhouse OP] TA414004

Warren House [3 pillboxes, AT blocks] TF445959

Toby's Hill, Saltfleet [disguised pillbox] TF456944

Seaview Farm [gun mount, 2 pillboxes, AT blocks & cylinders] TF462-5/924-8

Saltfleetby-All-Saints [4 pillboxes] TF452902, 452910, 448907, & 457905

Theddlethorpe-St-Helen [pillboxes] TF478902 [camouflaged as pig-sty] & 475891

Hogsthorpe area [Type 22 pillboxes] TF521739, 532716, 542715, 513738, 502711, 550737, & 547742 [two].

Jacksons Corner [remains of Coast Battery] TF573667

Gibraltar Point [2 pillboxes, OP, CASL position, AT blocks] TF550-65/577-84

Wrangle [3 pillboxes] TF459531, 460528, 459526

Butterwick [7 pillboxes] TF407437-420456

Freiston Shore [Coast Battery + 5 pillboxes] TF392406-398424

The Scalp, Boston Haven [two pairs of Type 26 pillboxes] TF389389, 396390

Boston Haven [6 pdr. gunhouse [now gazebo], pillbox, blockhouse] TF360-3/400

Holbeach-St-Matthew [blockhouse, 3 pillboxes, AT blocks] TF405-9/338-9

Sutton Bridge [Spigot Mortar Pedestal] TF487219

Coast Defence Chain Home Low Radar stations:

Donna Nook TF432989

Mablethorpe TF510850

Huttoft Bank TF539785

Chapel-St-Leonards TF565716

DEFENCE LINES [Chapter 3]

HOBHOLE DRAIN: Pillboxes TF382569, 379548, 374525, 366449, 370428, 368441, 367439, and at Freiston village: three Type 22 pillboxes TF 375436, 377437, 377436;

A16 LINE: Type 28a gunhouses for 6pdr. Hotchkiss QF guns, TF351583, 354566, 344583, & 369506, two destroyed at TF351516 & 3475651

GHQ LINE: Torksey Railway Bridge, AT rail sockets SK836792

RIVER WITHAM LINE: AT cylinders TFl 93570, 196561, pillbox SK926213

SOUTH FORTY FOOT DRAIN LINE: AT block TF249436, Type 22 pillbox TF175356

NEW RIVER ANCHOLME LINE: South Ferriby, Type 22 pillbox TA972210

TRENT & DOVE RIVER LINES: Confluence of Tame & Trent: three pillboxes SK191153, 189149, 193149. Railway bridge over Trent: 4 two-man pillboxes on bridge SK245210. Swarkestone Bridge: two spigot mortar pedestals SK371296, 368285. Shardlow pillbox SK441304. Melbourne railway bridge: AT blocks SK389274. Confluence of Trent, Dove & canal: 3 pillboxes SK279259, 268269, 268268. Former rail crossing of Dove: 2 pillboxes with sloping roofs SK24328718. Aston Bridge to Dove Bridge on A50: ten pillboxes at half-mile intervals. Ellastone Bridge: disguised gunhouse and elevated Type 22 pillbox SK1 2042314. Mayfield non-standard pillbox built into river-bank SKI59460

DEFENCE OF VULNERABLE POINTS [Chapter 4]

Nodal points and AT Islands

DERBYSHIRE

LEICESTERSHIRE: Ashwell/canal crossing: Type 22 pillbox SK865111. Gaddesby: spigot mortar pedestal SK688129. Ratcliffe-on-Wreake: 2 prefabricated square pillboxes SK623154, 628152. Redmile/Grantham Canal: Type 22 pillbox SK790355. Rotherby A607: spigot mortar pedestal & Home Guard store. Worthington: loophole inserted in 18C Lock-up SK408205

LINCOLNSHIRE: Boston: two Type 23 pillboxes TF327433 and one TF329436. Corby Glen/mainline railway: pillbox SK988251. Grantham. AT blocks at SK910356, 918349. Hatton Holegate: Type 22 pillbox TF417652. Horncastle: Type 22 pillbox TF244694. Lincoln: AT wall SK972272, AT rail sockets 981725, AT cylinders 961718. Shorts Corner: pillbox TF312529. Spalding. pillboxes TF231219, 229221, others gone, AT block TF229197. Spilsby: Type 22 pillboxes TF398661, 401659. Stamford: spigot mortar pedestal TFO27073

NORTHAMPTONSHIRE: Great Addington: loopholed wall SP959750. Nassington: Home Guard store TLO68962. Northampton: R. Nenel ex-Power-station 2 circular pillboxes SP76516/59617, loop-holed wall SP765581. Oundle: twin Home Guard stores TLO34883, spigot mortar pedestal 036881

NOTTINGHAMSHIRE: Kelham/R Trent: Type 22 pillbox SK775558. Stapleford/R. Erewash: Ruck pillbox SK478378. Trowell Moor: Type 22 pillbox SKS04403. Underwood: Type 22 pillbox SK483506

RUTLAND: Oakham: spigot mortar pedestal on Castle bank SK863090

Searchlight sites with pillboxes [* denotes Home Guard store]

DERBYSHIRE: Melbourne: SK371264. Stenson: SK319300. Firestone Hill SK337465

LEICESTERSHIRE: Asfordby: SK722215. Brickfield Farm: SK792154. Knipton: SK819300. Landyke Lane: SK740250. Melton: SK767206. Normanton: SK809405. Stathern Hill: SK775305. Witheote: SK788058

LINCOLNSHIRE Creeton: TFO13203. Crowland: TF268112. Holbeach: TL365212. Holbeach Drove: TF315109. Long Bennington: SK840457. Rochford: SK911304. Skillington: SK893257. *Sutton-St Edmund TF367118

NORTHAMPTONSHIRE: Brigstock: SK949860. East Carlton: SK824896. Gretton: SK904953. Pipeweil: SK840852. Rothwell: SP821802. Weldon: SP898851

NOTTINGHAMSHIRE: Arnold: SK605467. Costock Grange: SKS76208. Flintham: SK738455. Gotham: SK523302. Hose Lodge: SK718308. Vimy Ridge: SK668311

RUTLAND: Brooke: SK843053. Exton: SK920103. Greetham. SK945153. Ketton: SK992059. Lyndon: SK896052. Morcott: SK922002. Tixover: SK960011. Tolethorpe:TFO17109. Whissendine: SK840151

Other Vulnerable Points

DERBYSHIRE: Firestone Hill: radio station & SL site - two Type 22 pillboxes SK337463.

LEICESTERSHIRE: Launde Abbey: 44 AT cylinders; house may have been requisitioned.

LINCOLNSHIRE: Brackenborough Hall: two blockhouses TF330906; used as army HQ. Louth Park Farm: pillbox; Diver Operations Room. Orby radar site reputed to have pillboxes hidden by racetrack hoardings. South Witham: pillbox SK965195, former RAF [100MU] bomb dump. Stenigot radar site: 2 pillboxes TF256825, 255828 also Guardroom. Home Guard stores: Aubourn SK929628 Horbling TF115354 Louth

TF340849 Humberstone TA311054 Tattershall TF214578 Winterton SE933188

NORTHAMPTONSHIRE: Little Billing: guardpost on factory roof SP814616. Weedon Depot, loopholed quardpost inside main gate SP629597

NOTTINGHAMSHIRE: Nottingham: guardpost inside Castle gates SK569395; wartime HQ Watnall: blockhouse with 7 loops SK506454 + Type 22 pillbox SK507455; [formerly Fighter Command 12 Group Filter Room].

AIRFIELD DEFENCE [Chapter 5]

DERBYSHIRE: Ashbourne: BHQ noted in Action Stations 2 & Airfield Review 10.2, Oct '88. Burnaston. Airfield Plan, 1944, shows 11 pillboxes+ BHQ., pillboxes were FC Construction: all now destroyed. The airfield site is occupied by Toyota.

LEICESTERSHIRE: Bruntingthorpe. BHQ [11008/411] SP598895 Castle Donington: Type 22 pillbox SK445264. Market Harborough, BHQ [11008/41] SP718895

LINCOLNSHIRE: Barkston Heath: hexagonal pillboxes SK974418 & 965419. Binbrook: BHO [11008/41] TFI 84955; hexagonal pillbox TF206958. Coleby Grange: 2 loopholed entries to dispersal pens TF005611. Digby: hexagonal pillbox TF047562. others reported around perimeter. Goxhill: BHQ [11008/41] raised cupola TA108207. 0Ps [as named on AM Plan] composed of BHQ cupolas + Stanton shelters TA113223 & 1212211. Hibaldstow. BHQ [11008/41] SE979012. Manby: NB unique defended W/T block demolished. North Coates: 3 Type 23 [Lincs.] pillboxes buried in sea-wall TA368036, 371036, & 378026. Spitalgate: BHQ [11008/41] & hexagonal pillbox SK935353; 2 hexagonal pillboxes SK944353 & 950351; Allen-Williams Turret SK944354. Swinderby: BHQ [11008/41] raised on hillock SK886614. Wellingore: BHQ [11008/41] SK993546. 7 Type 22 pillboxes & 6 dispersal pens with loopholes, in continuous ring around airfield perimeter. Wickenby: BHQ [11008/41] TF103804

NORTHAMPTONSHIRE: Chipping Warden: BHQ L-shaped configuration of Stanton shelters with. Observation hatches, cabling etc. SP489499; FC Construction pillbox above ground SP495489. Croughton: FC Construction pillbox & two Seaqull trenches SP573332. Grafton Underwood: BHQ [11008/41] SP829810. FC Construction pillbox. SP929821, and another in ruins SP923807. Hinton-in-the-Hedges: BHQ [11008/41], two FC Construction pillboxes, and two Seagull trenches SP550372. hexagonal pillbox SP543374. Kingscliffe: BHQ [11008/41] & two FC Construction pillboxes TLO26972; two FC Construction pillboxes TL20978 & 021977,6 loopholed dispersal pens, surface air-raid shelters with roof LAA positions, & sewer-pipe LAA positions in continuous ring around airfield. PBX [5648/1] near Watch Office is a conversion of a BHQ [3329/41]. Polebrook: BHQ [11008/41] TL091872. Two hexagonal pillboxes with two loops in some faces TLO91872 & 093862. hexagonal pillbox TL097862. Sywell: BHQ in barn demolished. hexagonal pillbox SP817679, LAA pit for twin Lewis guns on Stork mount SP830682,

NOTTINGHAMSHIRE: Hucknall: BHQ [TG/1] three-storey brick tower, with associated Stanton shelters SK519475. hexagonal pillbox with 4 loops & porch SK528464 one-off hexagonal pillbox with 3 loops, open annexe to rear, & entrance protected by low blast-walls SK526463. Newton: octagonal pillbox SK673406. octagonal pillbox SK677405; rectangular, two-level pillbox SK678419; pillbox with two square, loopholed chambers, and central, open pit for LAA mount SK691413; rectangular pillbox with attached, open pit for LAA mount SK680415, octagonal pillboxes SK679406 & 686408. Ossington: BHQ [11008/41] SK740652. Tollerton: pillbox inside hangar SK616360; 9 octagonal pillboxes and 8 hexagonal, in continuous ring around perimeter of airfield;

RUTLAND: Cottesmore: hexagonal pillbox with open LAA platform attached SK900147, half-hexagonal pillbox built onto barn wall SK899146; North Luffenham: BHQ [11008/41] SK946043. stilted pillbox with 5 loops, built onto corner of 25 yard range, SK934046, Type 22 pillbox SK941055;

AIR DEFENCE [Chapter6J

ADBOLTON, Notts. WWII HAA site, magazine remains; SK604381

CLEETHORPES, Lincs. WWI air-raid shelter, Yarra Road; approx. TA309085

CLIPSTON, Northants. WWII Observer Corps. aircraft post. SP703827

ELVASTON, Derbys. HAA site, two gun positions, MT/workshop etc;SK4033326

EPWORTH, Lincs. WWII Observer Corps. aircraft post SE789045

GAUTBY, Lincs. control bunker for bombing decoy, TF164718

GRANTHAM, Lincs. HAA site, gun positions, magazines etc; SK944361

HUMBERSTON, Lincs: former CHL Radar station; TA330053

INGOLDMELLS, Lincs: former CHL Radar station; TF571697

KEELBY, Lincs. HAA site, part of 5.25 gun position + ?generator house; TA184117

LANGTOFT, Lincs. GCI Radar station, Happidrome etc. TF155130

MABLETHORPE, Lincs. ARP Reporting Centre TF510848
METHERINGHAM, Lincs. Railway Control Centre TFO77614
NEWARK, Notts. LAA Bofors tower SK794544
ORBY, Lincs. GCI Radar station TF526679
SKENDLEBY, Lincs. Chain Home Low & Extra Low Radar station; TF438708
SLEAFORD, Lincs. Maltings Water Tower, Observer Corps post, TFO75453
STENIGOT, Lincs. Chain Home Radar/GEE station, TF257825
SUTTON BASSETT, Northants: WWII Observer Corps aircraft post; SP770906
ULCEBY CROSS, Lincs. GEE station; TF406727
WARMINGTON, Northants, control bunker for bombing decoy; TFO82920
WATNALL, Notts. Fighter Command 12 Group Filter Room. SK506454

The DIVER FRINGE in Lincolnshire

HQ 41 AA Brigade, & Gun Operations Room,Louth Park Camp. TF349884
HQ 144[M] AA Regiment, South Elkington Hall; TF297882
HQ 24/9 AA Bty. The Camp, Marshchapel, [sites LA & LE] TF3599
HQ 25/9 AA Bty. Trusville Holiday Camp, Trusthorpe, [sites LF & LG]; TF515839 Troop 354169 Searchlight Bty. also at Trusthorpe,

HAA sites.

LA. RAF Northcoates TA370025
LB: Somercotes Haven TA409007
LC. Donna Nook TA431984
LD: Skidbrooke North End TA442954
LE: Toby's Hill TA449946
LF, Seaview Farm TA466922
LG: Sea Bank Farm TA478903; North End TA499868
LH: Bleak House TA492872
LI : Mablethorpe TF508853
H15: Humberston TA325066
H40: Low FarmTA379012

COLD WAR SITES [Chapter 7]

ROC/UKWMO SITES

ROC Midlands HQ: Fiskerton: TFO46725

ROC UNDERGROUND POSTS:

Alford TF410741 Buckminster SK873224

Burgh-on-Bain TF214841
Burton Joyee SK643445
Cold Overton SK806097
Collingham SK837629
Dunham-on-Trent SK822738
Epworth SE789045
Grantham SK903332
Harby SK745305
Holbeach TF364263
Louth TF337848
Melton Mowbray SK74121
Saxilby SK884792
Sleaford TFO74489
Spalding TF269213
Winterton SE935189

NB ORLIT 'A' aircraft post at BURGH-on-BAIN, & ORLIT 'B' at Swallow TA177024

ROTOR AA SYSTEM Radar sites:

Langtoft TFI 55130
Skendleby TF438708
Stenigot TF257825
Watnall sector control: SK506454;
Evaston AAOR [Derby GDA] SK403326

VHF Fixers:

Lutton TF464245 & Skidbrooke TF432948 [Uncs.] Beckingham SK775892 [Notts.]

THOR SITES Bardney, Caistor, Coleby Grange, Folkingham, Hemswell & Ludford Magna (Lincs. Harrington & Polebrook [Northants.] Melton Mowbray [Leics.] North Luffenham [Rutland]

BLOODHOUND SAM SITES Dunholme Lodge [Missile Assembly Building]: SK992780 North Coates, Woolfox Lodge.

ATOMIC WEAPONS STORES RAF Scampton: SK9680. Faldingworth PAD: TFO285. RAF Waddington: TFOO64

COMMUNICATIONS

Microwave Towers: Kirkby Underwood TFOS8273; Carlton Scroop SK956456; Claxby TF439708 Lincs. Copt Oak SK485127; Twycross SK303081; Leics. Oakham Radio Relay Station SK830088; Rutland Hill-top radio stations: Normanby-le-Wold TF115970; Kirkby U'w'd TFO58273; Fulletby TF301731 Lincs. Glebe Farm SK739035, Bardon Hill SK461132; Leics. Grange Farm SK501865; Alport Height SK305517-, Derbys. Robin Hoods Hills, Kirkby-in-Ashfield SK513552; Notts.

Other installations: Crowland, Lincs: TF262114 USAF radio relay station; Daventry Radio Station, Northants. SP587622 East Mere, Lines-. TFO13641, Cold War buildings on WWII listening post site; Kirton-in-Lindsey, Lincs: SK952980 USAF radio relay station; Spitaigate, Lincs: SK937345 USAF radio relay station,

BIBLIOGRAPHY

ALEXANDER, Colin. *Ironside's Line*, Historic Military Press. Storrington; 1999

BLAKE, R, HODGSON, M, & TAYLOR, B. *The Airfields of Lincolnshire since 1912*, Midland, Earl Shilton; 1984

BONSER, Roy. *Aviation in Leicestershire and Rutland,* Midland, Earl Shilton; 2001

BOWYER, Michael. *Action Stations 6. Military Airfields of the Cotswolds & Central Midlands*, PSL. Sparkford; 1983 & 1990

CADMAN, G. *20th Century Military Remains in Northants*, Northants. SMR. update

CADMAN, G. *Northants. Bombing Decoys*, Northants. Archaeology, 28; I998-99

CAMPBELL, D. *War Plan UK*, Burnett Books, London; 1982

CLOWES, Peter. *Peak District at War*, Churnet Valley Books, Leek; 2001,

COCKROFT, Wayne. *RAF Langtoft: Cold War Project Survey Report*, RCHME; 1998

COCROFT, Wayne. *Dangerous Energy*, English Heritage; 2000

COCROFT, Wayne., THOMAS Roger. *Cold War*, English Heritage; 2003

COLEMAN,EC. *The Royal Navy in Lincolnshire*, Richard Kay, Boston; 1991

DOBINSON, Colin. *AA Command*, Methuen/EH, London; 2001

DOBINSON, Colin. *Fields of Deception*, Methuen/EH; London; 2000

DOBINSON, Colin. *20th Century Fortification in England,* 12 volumes for Council for British Archaeology, [unpub. but copies with County SMRs] 1995-2000

DORMAN, Jeff. *Guardians of the Humber*, Humberside Leisure Services; 1990

DOWNES, M. *Oundle's War*, Nene Press, Oundle; nd

FRANCIS, Paul. *Control Towers*, Airfield Research Publishing, Ware; 1993

FRANCIS, Paul. *British Military Airfield Architecture*; PSL, Sparkford, 1996.

GIBSON, Michael. *Aviation in Northamptonshire*, Northants. Libraries; 1982

HALL, C E [ed]. *Look, Duck and Vanish,* Heritage Lincolnshire; 1996

HALL, G & FEARY, D. *HAGNABY The Dummy Airfield "W'Site*, Spilsby; 1995

HALPENNY, BB. *Action Stations 2. Military Airfields of Lincolnshire*

and the East Midlands, PSL, Sparkford; 1981
HANCOCK, T N. *Bomber County*, Lincolnshire Libraries; 1978
HANCOCK, T N. *Bomber County 2*; Lincolnshire Libraries; 1985
HARDY, C, & BROWN, R, *Derby at War*, Sutton, Stroud; 1998
HOGG, Ian. *Anti-aircraft Artillery*, Crowood; 2002
HOLLOWAY, B G & Banks, H. *Northamptonshire Home Guard*, NHG; 1949
HOLLOWELL, Steven. *Defending the Heart of England, Northampton 1940-44*. Northants Archaeology, 28, 1998-99
HURT, F. Lincoln During the War,. Li neol n; 1 99 1
INNES, G B. *British Airfield Buildings of 2nd World War*, Midland, Earl Shilton; 1995
INNES, G B. ditto, *Volume II*, Midland, Earl Shilton; 2000
JENKINS, R. *Leicestershire at War*, Sutton, Stroud; 1998
LOWRY, Bernard [ed]. *20th Century Defences in Britain*, CBA, York; 1995
McCAMLEY, N J. *Cold War Secret Nuclear Bunkers*, Leo Cooper, Barnsley; 2002 p
MOULD, Paul. *Wartime Schooldays in Boston*, Boston', 1996
NORTHANTS LIBRARIES. *Northamptonshire at War 1939-45*, Northampton; 1979
NOTTINGHAM. *Nottingham at War*, facsimile of WWII 1942 handbook; 1995
OSBORNE, Mike. *20th Century Defences in Britain: Lincolnshire*, Brasseys; 1997
PARKER, Charles. *The Royal Observer Corps in Lincolnshire*, Lincoln; nd
PILE, Gen. Sir F. *Ack-Ack*, Harrap, London; 1949
WILLS, Henry. *Pillboxes*, Leo Cooper/Secker & Warburg, London; 1985
WOOD, Derek. *Attack Warning Red*, Carmichael & Sweet, Portsmouth; 1976/1992

INDEX

Note: page numbers in bold type denote illustrations